A

SCANDALOUS

FREEDOM

ABOUT THE AUTHOR
Steve Brown

Steve Brown is a radio broadcaster, seminary professor, and author. He previously served as a pastor for twenty-five years and now devotes much of his time to the radio broadcast *Key Life*. Steve serves as professor of preaching at Reformed Theological Seminary in Orlando, Florida, and sits on the board of National Religious Broadcasters and Harvest USA. Traveling extensively, Steve is a much-in-demand speaker. He is the author of numerous books, including *Born Free, When Being Good Isn't Good Enough,* and *When Your Rope Breaks.* Steve and his wife, Anna, live in Florida.

STEVE BROWN

A SCANDALOUS FREEDOM

HOWARD
®PUBLISHING CO.

THE RADICAL NATURE OF THE GOSPEL

Our purpose at Howard Publishing is to:

- *Increase faith* in the hearts of growing Christians
- *Inspire holiness* in the lives of believers
- *Instill hope* in the hearts of struggling people everywhere

Because He's coming again!

A Scandalous Freedom © 2004 by Steve Brown
All rights reserved. Printed in the United States of America
Published by Howard Publishing Co., Inc.
3117 North 7th Street, West Monroe, Louisiana 71291-2227
www.howardpublishing.com

04 05 06 07 08 09 10 11 12 13   10 9 8 7 6 5 4 3 2 1

Edited by Steve Halliday
Cover design by David Carlson
Interior design by Gabe Cardinale

ISBN: 1-58229-392-9

CONTENTS

ACKNOWLEDGMENTS

I'm indebted to and thankful for . . .

. . . the people from whom I stole material (if I knew who they were, I would give them credit).

. . . those who have critiqued much of my teaching, some of whom did it out of love and some because they thought I was "ugly and my mother dressed me funny" (I learned from them both).

. . . my wife, Anna, who, in granting freedom to me and everybody she loves, has taught us more about the gospel than a book could ever teach.

. . . Reformed Theological Seminary, where I teach and where my colleagues keep me straight theologically (with varying degrees of success).

. . . George Bingham and the staff at Key Life Network, Inc. where I'm taught and given grace.

. . . my pastor Pete Alwinson, with whom I have shared the ideas of this book and who teaches me so much about grace.

. . . our daughter Robin DeMurga, who has been a wonderful editor and "mother" for this book, working with it from the beginning.

. . . our daughter Jennifer Robeson, sons-in-law Jim Robeson and Mike DeMurga, and our granddaughters Christy, Allison, and Courtney Robeson, who have all supported me in my ministry of radical grace.

. . . Steve Halliday, the best editor in America, for his gifted and sensitive editorial work and . . .

. . . the wonderful folks at Howard Publishing.

Without these people this book could have been far worse . . . but who knows? Maybe it could have been better.

INTRODUCTION

NAMING THE DEMONS

Seminary students are wonderful. I rejoice in being able to teach them. They wash out the soul of this old, cynical preacher.

Seminary students, however, have a tendency to feel quite sure about almost everything. I sometimes say to them, "Hey guys, you haven't sinned big enough or lived long enough even to have an opinion on that subject!"

Well, I've sinned big enough, and I've lived long enough to write a book like this one—and also to serve as the negative illustration of most of the principles taught herein. (Did you ever think that your sole purpose in life was to provide an illustration for others on how *not* to do it?) This is probably the only book I've ever written in which I am a true expert.

What follows may sound negative; but relax, it will seem like watching family movies. When we watch family movies, we identify with those on the screen because they are *us*. Even the simplest

1

things sound funny. It is my hope that by naming the demons in our family, those spirits will lose their power and we will be free.

So, are you ready? OK, here goes:

Some really wonderful people have lied to us.

They didn't mean to lie to us. (I know, because I've told some whoppers myself.) In fact, they had godly intentions and altruistic motivations. They didn't even know they lied. They wanted us to be more holy, more obedient, and more pious. They wanted us to have a clear and strong witness in the world. They hoped we would become lights on a hill.

But frankly, the light has gone dim, the day is far spent, and we are still religious, afraid, guilty, and bound.

Have you ever thought (but, of course, never said aloud) that somebody lied to you about being a Christian? Have you been a Christian for a long time and found that the promises given to you when you first "joined the club" have not come true? Even worse, you are required to act as if they have? Have you ever felt that someone changed the dictionary meanings for words like *freedom* ("Being free," they say, "means only that you're free to be good"), *grace* ("Grace is wonderful—but you shouldn't take advantage of it"), and *forgiveness* ("It's nice to be forgiven, but feeling sorry isn't enough")?

Bill Hendricks, in his very good book *Exit Interviews*, speaks about the impossible expectations on believers. He writes:

> Add it all up, and it's a crushing burden—absolutely staggering!
>
> Yet never have people been less able to live up to those expectations, biblically based though they may be. For one thing, we are not a morally or spiritually robust generation. It's not that we wouldn't love to live up to the high ideals with which we're challenged. But the fact is, we can't. They are so high and so many, and we are not only weak but in many cases wounded as well.
>
> The standard response to this fact is that, of course, we're weak as human beings, but with Christ's strength we can do "all things." With all due respect to that point of view, let me state

plainly that it's not going to happen that way. People are not going to become super-saints. They're going to live less than ideal lives, and lots of times they're going to fail. They're certainly not going to live up to anywhere near the heightened expectations of well-intentioned Christian teaching.[1]

I know whereof he speaks, because when I left the pastorate, the wheels had begun to fall off my wagon. Nobody knew it or even suspected it . . . but *I* knew.

I was recording five broadcasts a week; writing a book a year; traveling and speaking a hundred and fifty days a year; serving as an adjunct seminary professor; trying to be a good father, husband, and caring pastor; and, all the while, working at being a reasonably faithful Christian. And with all of the humility I can muster, I must say that I did all of those things quite well . . . and they were killing me.

Today I'm still doing many of those things—but now I'm doing them with a freedom and joy I never knew before. In this book I'm going to tell you why and how.

Martin Luther said that we must preach the good news to each other lest we become discouraged. That's what this book is about.

Jesus said we would know the truth and would be free indeed.

Let's see if he was right.

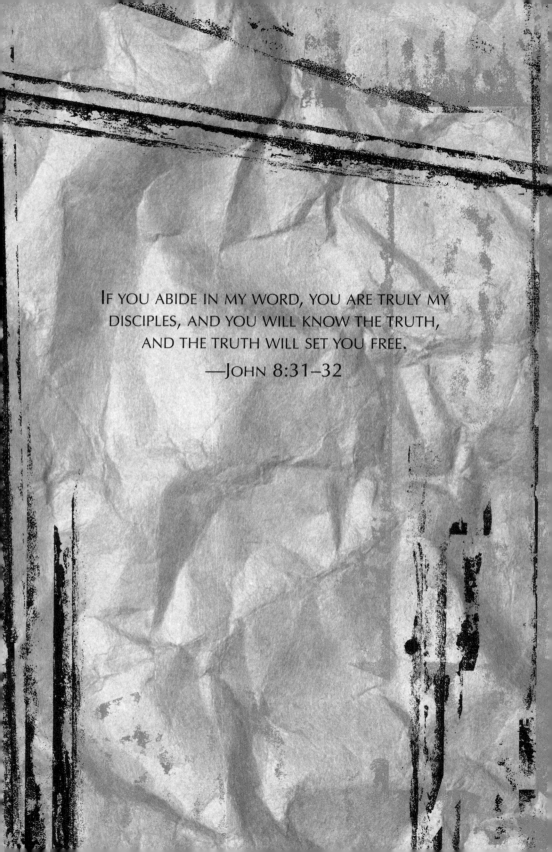

IF YOU ABIDE IN MY WORD, YOU ARE TRULY MY
DISCIPLES, AND YOU WILL KNOW THE TRUTH,
AND THE TRUTH WILL SET YOU FREE.
—JOHN 8:31–32

CHAPTER
ONE

THE FREEDOM WE SURRENDER . . .
and the Heritage That Sets Us Free

O, LORD, I WANT TO BE FREE, WANT TO BE FREE;
RAINBOW ROUND MY SHOULDER, WINGS ON MY FEET.
—TRADITIONAL SPIRITUAL

During the 2000 Democratic convention, someone commented that many of the views of the Democratic vice-presidential candidate, Joseph Lieberman, seemed not too distant from those of George W. Bush, the Republican nominee for president. Lieberman laughed. "That's like saying there is no difference between a taxidermist and a veterinarian, because in both cases you get your dog back."

Do you sometimes find a disconnect between what is supposed to be true and what really is? I do. Over the next few chapters, I want to talk about an area where that disconnect has grown probably as large as in any other area of the Christian life. The subject is freedom—and why we're not free.

FREE MEANS FREE

You've heard that Christ has made you free. You may have told others of your freedom. And you probably use the concept of freedom in your witness to those who don't yet know Christ. Sometimes, however, I fear that we define freedom in a way that restricts and binds more than it frees.

A lot of what we call freedom isn't real freedom at all. Furthermore, the similarity between real freedom and the freedom experienced by many Christians is the difference between the taxidermist and the veterinarian; while you do get your dog back, one collects dust while the other jumps, slobbers, and barks.

In a talk show that some friends and I broadcast for a number of months, we created a character named Edna and her husband, Orlo. (We got the idea from the late Jeff Carlson of WBCL in Fort Wayne, Indiana, a station that sometimes allows us to "steal" its ideas.) Edna and Orlo lived in a trailer and drove around the country, with Edna reporting on what they saw along the way. They also had a pet dog, Sparky, who had died. Instead of giving the dog a proper burial, they had Orlo's brother, a taxidermist, stuff him. So, wherever Edna and Orlo went, they took Sparky with them. In fact, Sparky became the hood ornament on their trailer.

I fear that much of the freedom Christians proclaim has the feel of a stuffed dog riding along as a hood ornament. It looks nice and is reminiscent of something once alive and vibrant, but it has become only a semblance of the real thing. The words and the connotations of those words—the outside—say one thing, but the reality and the substance—the inside—say quite another.

When Jesus used the word *free* (as in, "the truth will make you free"), he employed a term that means "liberation from bondage." In other words, the Greek word for *free* means "free." (Incidentally, the Hebrew word for *free* means "free" as well.) If you're looking for a dictionary definition, *free* means an "exemption or liberation from the control of some other person or some arbitrary power."

It ought to be that simple. If Jesus said we're free, we ought to accept his declaration at face value and run with it. It ought to help us define ourselves. But it doesn't. Christians will do almost anything to get away from the simple meaning of the word and the wonderful experience of freedom.

Something about freedom scares us to death. We continue in our bondage—and that is a major tragedy. It is a tragedy because Christ went to so much trouble to set us free. It is a tragedy because there is so much more to being a Christian than obeying rules, doing religious things, and being "nice." And it is a tragedy because our heritage is freedom . . . and we've sold it for a mess of pottage.

HOW WE STUFF THE DOG

Taxidermists have their methods, and not all ply their trade in the same way. The same is true of the way we mummify our liberty. Let me show you some of the ways we have "stuffed the dog" of freedom.

Free to Do Whatever We Want?

Many of us say, "As Christians, of course we're free—but that doesn't mean we're free to do whatever we want." But if we aren't free to do what we want, then we aren't really free. Or, if we are, it is a weird sort of freedom. Later I'm going to address some things that have to do with what we want, but for now I want to take the kicker away.

The Bible is quite radical; most of us don't understand just how radical it is. For instance, Paul writes, "I know and am persuaded in the Lord Jesus that nothing is unclean in itself, but it is unclean for anyone who thinks it unclean."[1] Again Paul writes, "Now the Lord is the Spirit, and where the Spirit of the Lord is, there is freedom."[2]

I have a friend who occasionally doesn't attend church.

Sometimes she doesn't have a quiet time and doesn't pray or read the Bible for a while. She will say, "It has become such a ritual and so empty of meaning, I just decided not to do religious stuff for a few days."

I like to kid her about her paganism; but others, I suspect, are just plain shocked. You know the type. They say, "How could you! After all that Jesus has done for you?" Or worse, they say, "If you aren't obedient to God, he won't bless you." If they feel *really* upset with my friend's freedom, they might even suggest that, if she doesn't get her act together, something really bad will happen to her. They love to quote Hebrews 12:6 about how God chastens those he loves.

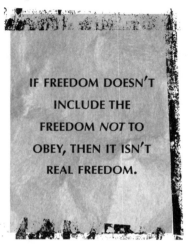

IF FREEDOM DOESN'T INCLUDE THE FREEDOM *NOT* TO OBEY, THEN IT ISN'T REAL FREEDOM.

They are implying that, if you don't go to church or if you miss your devotional time or if you don't read the Bible for too long, God will break your legs.

Do you know what she does? She laughs. That drives them up a wall.

Free to Sin?

Some reveal their flight from freedom in the comment, "Of course we're free, but that doesn't mean we're free to sin. It means we're free *not* to sin."

That sounds so very spiritual, and I believe there is something to it. In fact, I have the freedom to do some really good things I could never do before. I love more than I did, I am kinder than I was, and I sin less than I did. In one sense, doing wrong brings horrible bondage, while being free to live God's way brings genuine freedom.

Still, if that freedom doesn't include the freedom *not* to obey, then it isn't real freedom. Remember, Paul said, "For you were called to freedom, brothers and sisters; only do not use your freedom as an opportunity for self-indulgence."[3] He didn't want them to, but they could. Why? They were free.

A Christian does have an advantage over those who aren't Christians. Not only do we know the truth about what God wants us to do, he provides the power to do it. If we don't have the freedom not to do what he wants, however, we have redefined the word *freedom*.

Is Freedom Too Dangerous?

Sometimes we destroy freedom by saying, "We must be careful of this freedom thing. People will take advantage of it."

To them, I want to say, "What are you talking about, 'take advantage of freedom' by being free? Are you *crazy*? That's not freedom; that's a new kind of bondage."

I have a friend who, before he became a Christian, used foul language. He married a woman who didn't know such words, and he taught her how to curse. Shortly after they married, my wife and I had dinner with them. My friend took me aside and said, "Steve, don't go doing your Jesus thing at dinner. I like my wife just the way she is, and I don't want you to try to change her."

Years later my friend became a Christian and found himself bothered by the language of his still nonbelieving wife. He told her, "Honey, I know I taught you to talk that way, but would you watch your language?" She didn't understand what had happened and decided she could talk the way she wanted. And, yes, I restrained myself from reminding my friend that the problem could have been "fixed" years before if he had only let me do my "Jesus thing."

With a little spin, we do the same thing to new Christians. We teach them that they are free, but may God have mercy on their souls if they try to utilize what we taught them.

I remember a "mature" Christian admonishing a new Christian for dancing. "Can you imagine Jesus dancing?" asked the older lady.

"No," replied the new Christian, "I can't." Then, quite thoughtfully, she smiled and added, "I can't imagine him going to church, driving a car, or playing an organ either."

I'm sure the "mature" Christian straightened her out, but it ought to have been the other way around.

Will Freedom Hurt Our Witness?

In yet another way, we give freedom with one hand and take it away with the other. We like to tell believers that they are free—but if they utilize their freedom, they will hurt their witness.

A favorite verse usually goes with such counsel: "Therefore, if food makes my brother stumble, I will never again eat meat, lest I make my brother stumble."[4]

Without checking what the verse really means, the robbers of freedom make it into a horrible and condemning weapon. A misuse of that verse has caused more bondage than you can possibly imagine. We have taken away from Christians everything they could possibly enjoy because, in their enjoyment, they might hurt their witness.

The context of that verse deals with sacrifices to idols in a pagan society. Following the sacrifice, men took the meat to the downtown market and sold it. (What? Did you think the idols ate it?) Christians sometimes bought that meat, and the issue became whether or not a Christian could buy the meat and cook it on the backyard barbecue. Paul said that a Christian could freely do so. But because some uptight Christians (please note that he did not speak of unbelievers) might take offense, it would probably be better to have a salad rather than to give a brother or sister heartburn—even though the Christian remained free and the idols remained nothing. Even in light of this possibility, Paul refused to make a rule about total abstinence. He merely urged us to act wisely and considerately around fellow Christians.

I smoke a pipe. I also sometimes speak at very conservative gatherings of Christians. Do you think that, if I were the plenary speaker for the graduation banquet at Bob Jones University, I would yank out my pipe? No. But because I just told you that I smoke a pipe, some places will never invite me to come there and speak. And even if they did invite me, it would still be inappropriate for me to light up. Why? Not because we should never offend our brothers and sisters in Christ (we teach in our Born Free seminar that you ought to live your life with such freedom and joy that uptight Christians will doubt your salvation). It would be inappropriate because God says I should never act in such an unloving way that I might encourage members of my family to fall into sin through my example.

Suppose some fresh-faced underclassman saw me smoke my pipe, and although he still thought it wrong, he decided to give it a whirl anyway. In that case I have encouraged him to violate his conscience—to sin—through my expression of freedom. Paul does *not* teach us to refrain from the mere possibility of offending uptight brethren; he offended Christians left and right. And Jesus did so more than Paul.

(There is also the practical side about how smoking my pipe might affect the reception of my speech, to say nothing about my health.)

Let me ask you something: Do you know a single pagan who

stayed away from Christ because a Christian did not act as holy and as sanctified as he or she ought to have acted? I know they will say we're hypocrites—but usually that is just a smoke screen. The truth is, what repeatedly kills our witness is pretense, not freedom.

It would be so refreshing to say to our unbelieving friends, "I really mess up sometimes, but let me tell you something really good: God is still quite fond of me. Wouldn't it be great if you belonged to a God like that?" If we were that honest, the world would beat a path to our door.

YOU'RE FREE . . . REALLY FREE

The late Clarence Jordan, who in 1942 founded Koinonia Farms in Americus, Georgia, was also an accomplished Greek scholar. When he first moved to Americus, the Christian community heard of his Ph.D. in Greek and invited him to speak at a number of churches. I heard Dr. Jordan say that once they found out what he "really believed," the invitations dried up.

I strongly stand on what the Bible says about freedom, and while it may offend you, I can't change what the Bible says without leaving a smudge on the page. So, on the basis of what the Bible teaches, let me give you a radical statement:

You are really and truly and completely free.

There is no kicker. There is no if, and, or but. You are free. You can do it right or wrong. You can obey or disobey. You can run from Christ or run to Christ. You can choose to become a faithful Christian or an unfaithful Christian. You can cry, cuss, and spit, or laugh, sing, and dance. You can read a novel or the Bible. You can watch television or pray. You're free . . . really free.

Abraham Lincoln went to a slave market. There he noted a young, beautiful African-American woman being auctioned off to the highest offer. He bid on her and won. He could see the anger in the young woman's eyes and could imagine what she was thinking, *Another white man who will buy me, use me, and then discard me.*

As Lincoln walked off with his "property," he turned to the woman and said, "You're free."

"Yeah. What does that mean?" she replied.

"It means that you're free."

"Does that mean I can say whatever I want to say?"

"Yes," replied Lincoln, smiling, "it means you can say whatever you want to say."

"Does it mean," she asked incredulously, "that I can be whatever I want to be?"

"Yes, you can be whatever you want to be."

WHAT REPEATEDLY KILLS OUR WITNESS IS PRETENSE, NOT FREEDOM.

"Does it mean," the young woman said hesitantly, "that I can go wherever I want to go?"

"Yes, it means you are free and can go wherever you want to go."

"Then," said the young woman with tears welling up in her eyes, "I think I'll go with you."

That is what God has done for us. It is what the Christian faith is all about. We have been bought with a price, the price of God's own Son. We now have a new master, one who, once he paid the price, set us free.

If you've made it this far, I suspect you have some questions. So let's tackle them one at a time.

A Few Questions about Freedom

Does being free mean that, if I don't do what God says, he will still love me? Yes, that is exactly what it means. You might get hurt and regret what you've done, but you can do it and he won't stop loving you. You won't lose your salvation, and you won't get kicked out of the kingdom.

Does being free mean that God is pleased with whatever I do, no matter what it is? Of course not. Later in this book, we're going to talk about the law; but for now, let me give you a preview. God feels pleased when we do what he asks of us; but, because of the imputed righteousness of Christ,[5] he won't be angry with you nor will he ever condemn you.

Does being free mean that when Christians are really upset with me, God isn't? Yes.

Does being free mean that his love and grace are without condition . . . totally? Yes, that's exactly what it means.

What if I do something bad? Would God still bless me and answer my prayers? Yes, he will. What God does or does not do in your life rarely has anything to do with how good you are. Your teacher acts like that, not your God. In fact, I preached some of my best sermons when I was doing some bad stuff. God wanted to show me something very important. He demonstrated that his fondness for me depended on his love and the cross of Christ, not on my earning it.

Certainly there is something to be said for divine earthly retribution (you do bad stuff and bad stuff will happen to you) and divine earthly compensation (you do good stuff and good stuff will happen to you). That is the way the world generally works. God's laws shape the way the world operates. We do not break God's laws; we simply get broken by them.

If you are an unbeliever, let me give you some advice. Even if you don't believe there is a God, do what the Bible says God wants you to do. You will be a lot happier, have more peace, and possibly make more money than you do right now. Why will things probably work out this way? Because the Bible tells us the way things really are.

For the most part, however, those who preach a direct correlation between your goodness or obedience and God's blessing simply haven't read Psalms or looked around. I know obedient Christians who suffer in poverty and whose ministries have failed. And I know rich, peaceful pagans who are having a lot of fun.

The psalmist speaks to a reality that only the superficial will ignore:

> For I was envious of the arrogant when I saw the prosperity of the wicked. For they have no pangs until death; their bodies are fat and sleek. They are not in trouble as others are; they are not stricken like the rest of mankind. Therefore pride is their necklace; violence covers them as a garment. Their eyes swell out through fatness; their hearts overflow with follies. They scoff and speak with malice; loftily they threaten oppression. They set their mouths against the heavens, and their tongue struts through the earth. . . . All in vain have I kept my heart clean and washed my hands in innocence.[6]

Now the psalmist—and the entire Bible—has a lot more to say about the issue, but for now, let me repeat what I said before: If you are not faithful, God will not withdraw his blessing from you nor turn his back on you. God loves you and will bless you without condition, without reservation, and without equivocation.

You are free!

Something Attractive about Love

If you feel no attraction to a God who loves you without condition, then there is something wrong with you. I respond with love to those who love me. If someone likes me, I generally like him or her back. On the other hand, if someone is always judging, dishonoring, and criticizing me, then I want to get as far away as I can. But love? That's different.

There is something very attractive about love. It feels attractive to the same degree to which I am loved. Not only do I feel attracted to someone who loves me, I find myself wanting to please that person.

I was not the best student in the large high school I attended. In fact, I graduated fourth from the bottom in my class. But let me tell you about a teacher who cried when she gave me a low grade on a test. It really surprised me because I generally considered teachers the enemy.

This teacher returned our test papers and asked me to wait after class for mine. I figured I was in really big trouble. After everyone had left, she handed me my paper with a big F marked on it.

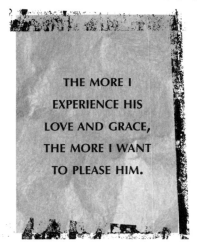

THE MORE I
EXPERIENCE HIS
LOVE AND GRACE,
THE MORE I WANT
TO PLEASE HIM.

"Stephen," she said, "you can do a whole lot better than this."

And then she started weeping.

I didn't know what to say or how to react. So I quietly left the classroom. Do you know something? I made an A on the next test. I didn't make that A because I had grown smarter or because I bought into academic excellence. I'm not that smart and, at that age, didn't care an ounce about academic excellence. I made an A because a teacher loved me enough to shed tears over my failure.

When Paul wrote to the church at Rome, he stood amazed at the rejection of God's love. "Or do you presume on the riches of his kindness and forbearance and patience," he writes, "not knowing that God's kindness is meant to lead you to repentance?"[7]

That is what God's goodness has done to me. It has created in my heart a great desire to please the one who loves me, knowing that, if I don't please him or even have the desire to please him, he will remain quite fond of me.

Sometimes I don't do it right. At times I get tired of being "religious" and don't do it. Other times I get so rebellious that even my mother, if she were still alive, would think about disowning me. But, dear friend, you have never met a man who wants to please God more than I do. The more I experience his love and grace, the more I want to please him.

BEWARE OF FREEDOM STEALERS

For the rest of this chapter, I want to talk about those who would take away your freedom. Of course, Satan wants to do this, but in this area, he works mostly through other Christians.

I once heard Sidlow Baxter say that whenever Satan gets to Christians, eight out of ten times, he does so through other Christians. Some people in the family of God will require things of you that God never required, will tell you that God is angry when he isn't, and will make you feel ashamed and guilty when you shouldn't feel ashamed and guilty.

It is important to remember I'm talking about my own family. I have robbed other Christians of their heritage of freedom so many times that I blush. But we have to talk—all of us. We need to get the first thing—the gospel—straight, or we are going to kill off one another. I'm trying to stop the carnage, and I don't want you to keep shooting either.

I once served as a character witness for a man who had done some really bad things. He was guilty as sin. His story appeared in the newspapers, got major play on all the television stations, and became the talk of the town. This man asked me to stand with him, and—this is a confession, in case you didn't notice—I thought about telling him of my frantic schedule and how I just couldn't do it. After all, I have a public media ministry, salaries to pay, and an image to maintain. So I had decided to buy out of this one . . . until

the Holy Spirit and my daughter, Robin, got together and forced me
to stand with my friend.

My friend was a member of a Pentecostal church. (A Pentecostal
is really different from a Presbyterian. You might say a Pentecostal
violates all the rules the Presbyterians make.)

At any rate, I found myself in the courthouse parking lot, talking
with a number of members of my friend's Pentecostal church. They
were surprised to see a Presbyterian in such a setting. I didn't tell
them I had almost stayed home. What I did tell them was this: "I'm
a Presbyterian, and we believe in a doctrine called 'radical and per-
vasive depravity.' If we find any depravity, however, we kick you
out." Those dear brothers and sisters laughed because they thought
I was joking. And I was . . . sort of.

New Christians come to our family, excited about their new-
found freedom and joy. Then we tell the new Christians that
while Jesus gave them something wonderful, they need to know a
few things. Then we put a saddle on that horse and ride it until
death. When the new Christians try to get out from under the burden of rules, regulations, and righteousness, we shame them into
continuing.

That makes me angry. It makes me angry when I've done it to
others, and it makes me angry when I see others doing it to me or to
my brothers and sisters in Christ.

It made Jesus angry too. He said of them, "They tie up heavy
burdens, hard to bear, and lay them on people's shoulders, but they
themselves are not willing to move them with their finger. . . . Woe
to you, scribes and Pharisees, hypocrites! For you travel across sea
and land to make a single proselyte, and when he becomes a proselyte, you make him twice as much a child of hell as yourselves."[8]

We've all played this freedom-robber role, and therefore none of
us can judge others. In fact, I believe that we show our depravity

less by the bad stuff we do than by our reversion to Pharisaism. It isn't our sin that is so bad (Jesus fixed that on the cross), but our stiffness. There's something about religion that can make you cold, critical, and mean. It's a tendency we have to fight all the time. I sometimes blush when I think of how often I have rained on a brother's or sister's parade.

FREEDOM'S POWER

Freedom has the power to take away, destroy, break down, and frighten. And it is this very power that we fear. While some of what follows may seem a bit harsh, please know that I'm not preaching. I am doing my best not to be self-righteous about the self-righteous. I don't want to be a Pharisee about Pharisees.

Freedom Takes Away Leverage

Freedom threatens religious people because it takes away their leverage and makes it more difficult for them to maintain control. They might want to maintain control for the right reasons, but they're still trying to be in control.

Jesus was not big into control. He said, "Whoever would be great among you must be your servant, and whoever would be first among you must be your slave, even as the Son of Man came not to be served but to serve, and to give his life as a ransom for many."[9]

One view in the church (and I still struggle with it) says that Christians have a tendency to be wild, and if we don't do something to maintain control, they will . . . well, get out of control.

One time, Abraham Lincoln was plowing behind a mule that had a horsefly on its rump. Lincoln's brother came along and flicked off the biting insect. "What did you do that for?" demanded Lincoln. "That was the only thing that made him go."

Sometimes we think that the only thing that will make a

Christian "go" is a bit of fear and guilt. Of course, Jesus has forgiven their sins—but how can we possibly tell them? They'll take it way too far, for sure.

Freedom Takes Away Power

Freedom also threatens religious people because it takes away their power. Yet even if we want to maintain power for the right reasons, it is still power and can rob us of freedom.

"But we do need authority," we object. "Without legitimate authority, discipline, and a proper chain of command, anarchy ensues, and everything for which Christ died will come crashing down around our feet."

Jesus wasn't terribly happy with such a view. "You know that the rulers of the Gentiles lord it over them, and their great ones exercise authority over them," he said. "It shall not be so among you."[10]

Freedom Destroys Smugness

Freedom scares religious folks to death because a lot of ego goes into being right and "righteous." If we aren't right and good, how do we differ from those other Christians who always get it wrong?

It always amazes me how irritated those of us who are right and righteous become when we get around those who *think* they are right and righteous. I don't have to be other people's mother, but I certainly want to be. And I think, *If I give them freedom to be what God wants them to be, where will I be?* So, I don't give them freedom.

Paul said, "Who are you to pass judgment on the servant of another? It is before his own master that he stands or falls."[11]

Self-righteousness is one of the most addicting things in the world. You'll find it rampant in Hollywood, in the halls of Congress on both sides of the aisles, in the books that try to politicize us, and in the arrogance that every crime brings to those who read about it in the newspapers or see it on television. You will find it on every street corner and in every home. But the one place you should have trouble finding it is in the church, where the bad people are supposed to find love.

Let me tell you something important. The abortionists make me so angry that sometimes I can hardly control it. The pornographers and purveyors of filth ought to be put in jail and the key thrown away. Racists and exploiters, those who hurt the innocent and the poor, irritate me to the point of revolutionary fervor. I hate how churches rob people of their freedom. I hate the liberals who pretend to believe but don't, and have, as a result, damaged the Christian faith. I want them all gone.

> FREEDOM SCARES RELIGIOUS FOLKS TO DEATH BECAUSE A LOT OF EGO GOES INTO BEING RIGHT AND "RIGHTEOUS."

And, yes, I'm making a point, but it isn't the one you probably think.

It felt *good* to write all that. Something in me, a smug self-righteousness, causes me to feel wonderful when I condemn others.

I don't drink alcoholic beverages, and so I have a great sermon on abstinence. In fact, if you heard me preach it, you would feel quite impressed with its power and conviction. I can't preach it, however. Jesus simply won't let me. He let me know that I liked the sermon too much.

We all have sermons we like too much.

Freedom Breaks Down Walls

The thought of freedom displeases a lot of Christians because they think we must maintain a clear demarcation between us and them.

In order to maintain that demarcation, we must have discipline and conformity. After all, what would happen if we couldn't tell the difference between the good guys and bad guys? If we don't stop talking about this freedom thing, we will get lost in the crowd and lose our witness.

Maybe. And then again, maybe not.

Jesus seemed to suggest that mustard seeds and leaven often go unnoticed, and furthermore, in the end, God will sort it all out.[12]

I have a friend on dialysis. Three times a week he has to go to a dialysis center to cleanse his blood. That process keeps him alive. I asked my friend what he did when he was traveling. He told me that he just skipped the procedures.

"Can you *do* that?" I asked.

"Oh yes, and I do fine," he replied with a laugh. "The problem is that the people at the center say it's risky. I think, however, that it's more risky to their bottom line than it is to my health. I pay them seven hundred dollars for each treatment, and the risky thing to them is that when I miss, they don't get their money."

Some of us in control may redefine freedom for the right reasons, but I suspect a lot of it has to do with another agenda. If we allow followers to live free, we risk a lot. I think, however, it puts more at risk our agenda of power and control and our need to be right and righteous, than it does those who need protection from the "dangers" of freedom.

Freedom Scares Us

We often find it easy and tempting to blame our loss of freedom on others when, in fact, we simply don't want to be free. Freedom scares us because we don't trust ourselves.

We find it comforting to have others decide for us. If we're free, we could be wrong—and we don't want to be wrong. That's the essence of perfectionism: If I haven't done it wrong, I'm still perfect; and even if I do it wrong when someone else told me to do it wrong, that takes away from their perfectionism, not mine.

Besides, living in a prison cell can bring real comfort. You may not like it a lot at first, but eventually you grow accustomed to the darkness. After all, the sunshine might hurt your eyes.

A friend of mine sent me a wonderful story from her local newspaper.[13] It told about a priest, the Reverend Thomas J. Quinlan, a seventy-one-year-old "chain smoker with a voice like sandpaper" who seems to go out of his way to offend folks.

"He once rode down the center aisle of the Basilica of Saint Mary of the Immaculate Conception in Norfolk on a police motorcycle for a Palm Sunday procession." Another time he dressed like Superman during a worship service in order to make a point. They try to keep Quinlan in line, but he will have none of it. He doesn't like "playing footsie with authority," and he hates the trappings of power.

The funny thing about Reverend Quinlan is that the churches he serves keep growing. In fact, one church he served tripled both in attendance and giving. Everywhere Quinlan serves, the members of the church become involved in ministry. So, despite his funny ways, God is doing something through him in a wonderful and delightful way.

Last year Quinlan, who has struggled with alcoholism for many years, was arrested for drunk driving. He went to his congregation and confessed, telling them that he would leave willingly. But all along he had set them free and taught them well. Do you know what they said to him? "We don't want you to leave; we want you to change." Those dear folks, the reporter said, "loved him into sobriety."

That's it! They've got it.

I just wish he had been a Presbyterian.

Hit Any Key

When I first started using computers to write, I used Wordstar. Most of you have no idea that Wordstar was one of the first word-processing programs. It had no pull-down menus, and it was necessary to memorize a lot of keystrokes in order to make it work. For years it remained the only widely used word-processing program, and almost everyone had to learn it.

A tutorial program on Wordstar tried to help neophytes like me get over our fear of computers. The opening screen featured a little man standing there and smiling. The caption read: "I bet you think if you do the wrong thing, hit the wrong key, or make a mistake, you could blow up the computer?"

The next screen showed the same little man saying, "Go ahead. Hit any key and see what happens." After you hit a key, a gigantic explosion glowed on the monitor. Moments later the same little man reappeared, smiling again and saying, "Just kidding!"

I love watching Christians become free; it's one of the great things about the ministry God has given me. Sometimes I have a hard time convincing them, but I understand their hesitation.

Freedom can be a hard road to walk.

At times I feel like that little man in the Wordstar program. I say, "Bet you think if you were free, you would blow up everything. Bet you think if you were free, you would lose control and have no power. Bet you think if you were free, the work of God would stop—and he *so* needs your help."

Go ahead. Be free the way Jesus told you.

You'll be really glad.

No one has ever seen God; the only God, who is at the Father's side, he has made him known.

—John 1:18

CHAPTER
TWO

THE GODS WE WORSHIP...
and the God Who Sets Us Free

THE GOD OF THE CANNIBALS WILL BE A CANNIBAL, OF THE
CRUSADERS A CRUSADER, AND OF THE MERCHANT, A MERCHANT.
—RALPH WALDO EMERSON

Do you remember the God Is Dead movement? A number of prominent theologians such as Thomas Altizer, William Hamilton, Gabriel Vahanian, Paul van Buren, et al pronounced God dead, so we had to make it on our own.

As you can imagine, the movement generated quite a bit of controversy. Every newsmagazine in America, in one form or another, did a cover story on it. Television specials, public debates, and symposiums on college and university campuses across the country dealt with the divine demise.

Then, as quickly as it began, the God Is Dead movement died. I suppose most folks just couldn't deal with the implications of a meaningless universe. Boiled down, those implications amounted to this: If there is no God, there is no value; if there is no value, there is no meaning; and, if there is no meaning, you are a turnip growing for a time, dying, and returning to the earth from which you came.

I believe the God Is Dead movement died too quickly. I think a lot of gods deserve to die. And in this chapter, I want to tell you about them.

A CRUCIAL QUESTION

Every thinking person ought to have a list of life questions. At the top of that list ought to be a question about God and his existence.

I'm constantly amazed at the people who never even consider it or who accept, without question, their parents' or their culture's theism or atheism. That's tragic, because if there is a God, he's in charge; if there isn't, then you are. And what you believe or don't believe about God has profound implications for your freedom.

You say you already believe God exists and that he is in charge? Then a second question demands an answer: If God exists, what is he like? What you believe about God's nature will largely determine how you live.

Almost all the inane things Christians do to remain bound and "religious" ultimately funnel down to what they believe about God. Many of us don't live free because we don't believe in a God who loves us enough to give us the gift of freedom.

If we deduced the nature of God from those who say they worship him, we would never believe he could be the God who sets people free. We would think God was against freedom, violently opposed to laughter, and very, very serious. We might also think he was angry at those who weren't very, very serious. If we looked at his people, we would think that God had adopted our political/cultural agenda and frowned on anything that violated it. If we looked at us before we looked at him, I'm afraid that our prisons would be more apparent than our freedom.

While I don't want to spend a lot of time behind bars, let me describe three idols that we create and worship—the gods who rob us of our freedom and joy.

God As Santa Claus

No doubt you know many Christians who worship the magical, Santa Claus god. They always try to appear happy, always praise Jesus, and seem breathtakingly quick with the clichés . . . until something really bad happens.

It amazes me how often we Christians bring our agenda to God, expecting him to bless and honor it, and then feel devastated when he refuses to play our little game.

A dream recently died on me. I thought it was God's dream.

The death especially hurt because I had hoped for and cherished the dream for almost fifteen years. While I won't go into details, the dream concerned an edgy, postmodern radio show that would reach out to listeners not open to anything traditional having to do with God. It was a very good dream, my motives were proper, and God allowed me to live it for two and a half years.

I figured this dream would fully blossom. We broadcast the show in ten markets and seemed to be doing quite well. Yet we had a problem. We needed twenty markets to make the show commercially viable—and we attracted only half the number required. No one else would risk the controversy.

So, after two and a half years, a whole lot of money, and the involvement of many people who also thought my dream was God's dream, the show went down in flames. I don't mind a dream dying, if it dies quietly without anyone noticing. (I once dreamed of being an evangelist like Billy Graham or a scholar like J. I. Packer. Nobody knew about those dreams, and when they died, they died quietly and privately. That's best.) This dream, however, expired publicly in front of a large audience. The embarrassment reached . . . well, embarrassing levels. Everywhere I went people asked me about the new show and how it was going. Countless times I had to relate the failure of my dream.

I pleaded with God about it. I told him how much he needed the new show and what great honor it would bring to him. I said to him, "Lord, if you really, *really*, loved me, you would make this thing successful." (God must laugh when we tell him our plans.) I finally realized that I didn't get a vote, that God was sovereign, and that I needed to accept his will. I asked him to give me release, closure, and joy in whatever he decided. God did—but I would rather have seen the dream realized.

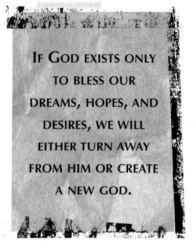

IF GOD EXISTS ONLY TO BLESS OUR DREAMS, HOPES, AND DESIRES, WE WILL EITHER TURN AWAY FROM HIM OR CREATE A NEW GOD.

The death of a dream is a minor thing. The kingdom, the world, and my life aren't going to vastly change because of a radio show. There are things of far greater importance.

But what if your dream defines your life, and it doesn't work out the way you thought it would? What if it has to do with a physical or emotional disability? What if your dream concerns your marriage, your children, or your business? What if your dream, your hopes, and your requests of God encompass things far more important than a radio show?

If you worship a little god of your own creation or a god who always says yes to your prayers, always blesses your agenda, and always makes you healthy, wealthy, and wise, then you have a serious problem. Throngs of Christians live with discouragement, bitterness, and anger simply because they worship a god who never existed.

In the foreword to his very good book *Disappointment with God,* Philip Yancey writes:

> I found that for many people there is a large gap between what they expect from their Christian faith and what they actually experience. From a steady diet of books, sermons, and personal testimonies, all promising triumph and success, they learn to expect dramatic evidence of God working in their lives. If they do not see such evidence, they feel disappointment, betrayal and often guilt.[1]

What a Christian does as a result of broken dreams, shattered hopes, and unfulfilled desires depends on what he or she believes about God. If God exists only to bless our dreams, hopes, and desires, we will either turn away from him or create a new god.

God As a Child Abuser

When our dreams shatter, we tend to create a child-abuser god. This god makes everything you enjoy either sinful or fattening. He never says yes and takes great delight in messing up your life—all for your own good, of course. This god gives AIDS to those who displease him with their sexual immorality, cancer to those who haven't lived up to his wishes, and failure to those who dare to step out of line.

A friend of mine is a malpractice lawyer. He isn't *just* a malpractice lawyer either; he is a *very successful* malpractice lawyer. He has won multimillion-dollar judgments from all sorts of companies. Now, he hasn't enjoyed such success by being a weenie. He is strong, in your face, and frighteningly articulate.

I remember when he became a Christian. (Oh yes, one can be a Christian and a flourishing malpractice attorney—but it isn't easy!) My friend went about his new faith with the same determination that he used to sue insurance companies. He started reading the book of Genesis and would have finished the entire Bible in one sitting, if not for his day job.

One day he visited my office. "Steve," he said, "I've been reading the Bible, and God isn't who I thought he was. He's killing off entire cities and cattle and women and children . . ." Then he stopped and smiled. "Don't get me wrong," he continued. "He's my kind of guy."

My friend knows more now because he has read the entire Bible. His false initial impression of God's nature, however, runs rampant in Christian circles. I even have a pastor friend whose church accused him of being out of the will of God when his wife gave birth to a stillborn child. The people in his congregation didn't intend to be mean; I suppose they were trying to help. But it still makes me angry.

We're going to see later how belief in this kind of God gives others the power to manipulate us through guilt. But for now, let me say that if you believe in such an ogre god, you will live in perpetual fear of offending him. If you worship the "god of the lightning bolts," you won't laugh much, you will hesitate to dance and sing, and you will never risk anything. If you worship a God who is out to get you, you will never be free . . . free to cuss and spit, free to move to joyous acceptance, and free to get on with your life.

Dan Allender and Tremper Longman, in their book *Cry of the Soul: How Our Emotions Reveal Our Deepest Questions about God,* tell about a girl they call Maria. Maria's brother had sexually abused her over a period of eight years. Worse, he often "sold" her to his friends. The abuse stopped only when he died in an automobile accident. When Maria told her mother about the long years of torment, the angry woman replied that it was a lie and said that if Maria ever spoke of it again, she would no longer be her daughter.

Maria illustrates what is at the heart of despair—a flight from desire. Desire so often proves fruitless. Disappointment has answered hope so many times that it seems utterly absurd to continue to hunger or yearn for anything any longer. To hope is to become vulnerable to more pain. The best solution, therefore, seems to be to completely shut down, become robot-like, and expect absolutely nothing out of life.[2]

Have you met Christians like these? Have you found yourself languishing under such idolatry? These Christians remain continually serious, deeply frightened, and make every effort to get you to become more serious and more frightened. They talk about hell more than heaven and God's requirements more than his grace. They feel utterly miserable.

Too many of us have come to believe in a God who is a child abuser, a God who demands that we go through hell to get to heaven. We may not say it, but our actions do. We live with the attitude of, "You pagans, go ahead and have your fun, but you're going to get yours. I may be miserable, uptight, critical, and bound now, but I'm going to get a crown someday. And you're going to roast." We believe that pagans get to go through heaven to get to hell, but God will fix everything in the end. We'll get paradise, and they'll get the lake of fire.

I suppose that kind of nonsense might turn out OK. We could get to heaven and find out we had made a terrible mistake, but at least we would be in heaven and finally free. What a loss though. Martin Luther's fondness for beer is well-known. He is reported to have once said, "God made beer to show that he loves us and wants us to be happy." Now, I'm a teetotaler. I just can't get that stuff down. But I know what Luther was saying, and if you were offended, you may desperately need this book.

If God is really a monster, then when bad stuff happens to me, I will become more bound, enslaved, and angry. If, on the other hand,

I understand that God is my Father, that he loves me without reservation, and that he knows exactly what he is doing, I will learn how to live in freedom. I might get angry at first and shake my fist at him. I might sputter and resist, but in the end, I will run to him and will (eventually) be able to accept his way in my life, and do so with joy and freedom.

The Absent God

When you try and fail to worship a god who can't be pleased, then you often create a god who has gone away on vacation to Bermuda. This is the god of deism, quite popular in the eighteenth century.

But deism always suffered from an intellectual shallowness that couldn't support the weight of numerous objections. (Consider this a sort of have-your-cake-and-eat-it-too idol. Voltaire and others simply couldn't maintain their propositions against the very cogent charge that if God has left the building, he might as well not exist.)

Heresies have a tendency to repeatedly resurface, however, and this one keeps appearing in the lives of Christians who can't please the child-abuser god and can no longer worship at the altar of the Santa Claus god.

Oh, the people who worship this idol don't claim to be deists. In fact, most don't even know what a deist is. But for all practical purposes, that is what they are. They often wear the mask of Calvinism. A misunderstanding of the sovereignty of God can make us philosophical determinists who see human beings as automatons at the mercy of mindless forces of nature, genetics, or circumstances. Some call this "god."

The late British philosopher Bertrand Russell made his views of God very clear. He didn't believe in one; or if he did, he hid the fact quite well. I suspect (but certainly don't know) that he disbelieved in God because—as seen in his 1929 book, *Manners and Morals*—he had a bone to pick with God's ideas about sex. Whatever the case, no one doubts that Russell was a philosophical atheist or something close to it.

An interviewer speaking with the aged philosopher began a question with the words, "Dr. Russell, as an atheist—"

Russell interrupted the man, loudly protesting, "I've never said that I didn't believe in God. I said that I wasn't sure."

I believe that Russell was cramming for finals. He knew that death awaited him just around the corner, and I suspect that the last thing he wanted to do just before meeting God (should he exist) was to say that he didn't exist. In that

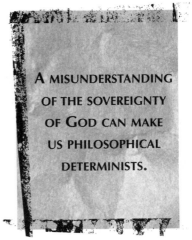

A MISUNDERSTANDING OF THE SOVEREIGNTY OF GOD CAN MAKE US PHILOSOPHICAL DETERMINISTS.

sense, Russell differed little from a lot of folks who have become practical deists. They believe that after God made the rules of the universe, he wandered off. Still, they don't want to say so . . . especially in thunderstorms.

The problem with the uninvolved, uncaring, unfeeling god is that he tends to make one uninvolved, uncaring, and unfeeling. This most miserable of all theological views robs one of passion. The wonderful book *The Sacred Romance* describes the worshiper of the deist idol:

> In our modern, pragmatic world we often have no such mentor [referring to Eli's mentoring of Samuel in regard to hearing God's voice], so we do not understand it is God speaking to us in our heart. Having so long been out of touch with our deepest longing, we fail to recognize the voice and the One who is calling to us through it. Frustrated by our heart's continuing sabotage of a dutiful Christian life, some of us silence the voice by locking our heart

away in the attic, feeding it only the bread and water of duty and obligation until it is almost dead, the voice now small and weak. But sometimes in the night, when our defenses are down, we still hear it call to us, oh so faintly—a distant whisper. Come morning, the new day's activities scream for our attention, the sound of the cry is gone, and we congratulate ourselves on finally overcoming the flesh.[3]

At least the believer in the Santa Claus god can laugh and sing. It may be a silly way to feel about god, but it is a real feeling.

At least the child-abuser god solicits some kind of action. A man or woman who learns to swim in a pool of alligators may swim only because he or she fears the alligators, but he or she does swim.

Sadly, believers in the deist idol do nothing. Like lemmings, they make their way to the ocean and jump to their deaths without a thought about life.

Better to get angry at God than to simply accept what is without either a profanity or a whimper. It may sound heroic, but really it's only sad.

STRUGGLING WITH THE TRUTH

If the bad stuff in life comes from (or is allowed by) a monster God, I will continue to seethe with anger. If the bad stuff comes from a weenie God, I will tell him that he is wrong and that I won't have anything to do with him anymore. But if the bad stuff comes from a loving and sovereign Father, at some point I will rejoice and be free.

Do you want to be a street-smart Christian? Then determine the nature of reality and act in a manner consistent with it. God's nature is what it is, not what we think it is or what we hope it is. Therefore, if we want to live free, we have to find out what God is like, and then act accordingly.

But don't expect freedom to come without a struggle.

Until a Christian struggles with the issue of freedom, he or she will remain frightened, obsessive, and bound. One *has* to struggle. Before we look at some answers about God's nature and ponder how our view of his nature affects our lives, let's struggle a bit.

I suspect that, before we finish this chapter, you will wish that I would just get to the bottom line and ignore all of the theological stuff. But when we fail to deal with basic theological and biblical truths—when we know only that "Jesus loves me, this I know"—we *won't* truly know that Jesus loves us, and we *will* continue to worship an unreal god.

Did you hear about the astronomer and the pastor who flew on a plane together? The astronomer asked the pastor what he did for a living. When the pastor told him, he replied, "Reverend, I keep my religion simple: Jesus loves me, this I know."

The pastor then asked the astronomer what he did. Upon finding out, he smiled and declared, "Oh, I keep my astronomy simple: Twinkle, twinkle little star."

Someone has said that simplicity on this side of complexity is worthless, but simplicity on the other side of complexity is worth anything you had to pay to get there.

So—let's struggle on this side of complexity. I suggest that we start with a reality that can really hurt.

The Dark Side of Appearances

When a mother who lived in a country not yet reached with the gospel first heard of God's love and grace, she said, "I always knew there must be a God like that somewhere." She thus expressed the expectation that somewhere a kind and benevolent God had to exist.

But unless you are living a Christian life of denial (and we're going to talk about that later), you know that many pieces of evidence suggest that the God who is, does not always look as benevolent and as kind as we would like.

Suppose that someone had told this woman about a vindictive, angry, abusive God? Given the pain that all of us face, the tragedy in our lives, the hardship in the lives of those we love, the silence of God, and the harshness of our experiences, I believe she could just as well have said, "I always knew there *must* be a horrible God like that."

This morning I answered a letter from a father whose sixteen-year-old son just died from a drug overdose. The man said that he had become a Christian as a result of my radio teaching. He had read my books to help him through a difficult time. He told me he always felt, no matter how bad it got, God would not give him more than he could bear.

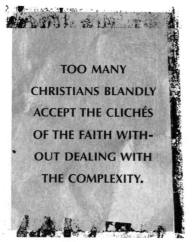

TOO MANY CHRISTIANS BLANDLY ACCEPT THE CLICHÉS OF THE FAITH WITHOUT DEALING WITH THE COMPLEXITY.

"But, Steve," he wrote, "I can't bear *this*. I pleaded with God. I begged him. I asked him to give me a sign. He didn't even budge. I'm through with this God stuff."

I understood at least part of this man's pain and questions. I've felt the pain too. I have asked all the questions he is now asking. I've cleaned up after more suicides than I can remember and stood by more deathbeds than I can count. I've listened to and made so many confessions, tried to help when there was no help, tried to fix the unfixable so many times, that I've often wanted to be through with this "God stuff" too.

I believe that too many Christians blandly accept the clichés of the faith without dealing with the complexity. *Jesus loves me, this I know, for the Bible tells me so* is fine until the doctor tells you that you have cancer, your business goes down in flames, or your spouse leaves you for someone more beautiful, compassionate, or understanding. It's nice to "tiptoe through the tulips with Jesus" until your child dies, your abuse comes rushing back in a torrent of horrible memory, or you feel that your pain will kill you. It's hard to find Jesus among the tulips when you walk through bleak, cratered landscape.

I know that sounds depressing; in fact, I designed this book to help with that depression. But if we don't talk about this issue, we aren't going to get anywhere. So, whatever you do, don't put this book down until you finish this chapter. You might not agree with everything that lies ahead, but at least hear me out.

A Quest for the Real God

A multitude of intellectual and rational justifications support the premise that a good God remains in charge of this mess.

If you have trouble believing in a benevolent and sovereign God, I suggest that you go to any Christian bookstore or library and do some research. There you should find some intellectually satisfying answers to the questions that thinking people always have asked about a benevolent God in a less-than-benevolent world.

But that isn't our real problem, is it?

I often tell those who are suffering through very painful circumstances and who have asked me why that the intellectual answers they seek won't help much. I sometimes say, "You have a broken heart, not a broken head. When the pain dissipates, we'll talk about some answers to the problem of pain. What you need now is 'heart medicine,' not a logical syllogism."

My friend, the recording artist Betty McDaniel, says that the mind believes only what it has learned, but the heart believes only what it has experienced. If our experience has highlighted pain, unless we have another experience of the heart, we will believe in an abusive God who has inflicted that pain.

Now, let me tell you something I've discovered from many years as a teacher and pastor. I've found that most of the ideas we have about God arise from a visceral rather than a cerebral source. In other words, most of us don't look at the facts, check the Bible, and really think. To the contrary, most of us draw our idea of God from the experiences (good or bad) of our lives. But the issue is far too important to rely on such an unthinking treatment.

If we want to know about the real God, only one source will do.

Look to Jesus

Biblical Christians should find out about God from Jesus. Christ is the standard for everything a Christian should think about God.

If something we think about God violates what we know of Jesus, what he taught, and how he acted, then that thought lies. If someone gives us the impression that God's nature differs from what Jesus said and demonstrated it to be, then don't buy a used car from that person—and don't listen to anything he or she says about anything else. If someone errs on this important issue, probably he or she will go badly wrong about a whole lot more.

What I'm about to say isn't wish fulfillment, a hopeful doctrine, or anything of the sort. It's a fact—a space/time fact—that God took on human flesh and lived for a while in our presence. Throughout history people like you and I have asked our questions about God. Is there really a God? Did he create all of this? Does he care? Does he love? Does he love *me*? Somebody always gave answers to such questions, but most of them amounted to little but conjecture— head answers to the heart's questions. Then, in a breathtaking and explosive way, God moved into our hearts—not with propositions, but with himself.

"In the beginning was the Word," the apostle John writes, "and the Word was with God and the Word was God. He was in the beginning with God. All things were made through him, and without him not any thing made that was made. . . . And the Word became flesh and dwelt among us, and we have seen his glory, glory as of the only Son from the Father, full of grace and truth."[4]

Again John wrote: "That which was from the beginning, which we have heard, which we have seen with our eyes, which we looked upon and have touched with our hands, concerning the word of life—the life was made manifest, and we have seen it, and testify to it and proclaim to you the eternal life, which was with the Father and was made manifest to us."[5]

The book of Hebrews opens with these words: "God, who at various times and in various ways spoke in time past to the fathers by the prophets, has in these last days spoken to us by His Son, whom He has appointed heir of all things, through whom also He made the worlds; who being the brightness of His glory and the express image of His person, and upholding all things by the word of His power."[6]

Do you want to know what God is like? Then look at Jesus. If you want to know how God reacts to people, look at how Jesus reacted to people. If you want to know what God thinks, how he acts and who he is, don't get with a group of people and vote on it. One doesn't discover divine truth with an election. If you want to know the truth about God, don't get a book on theology, listen to a preacher, or even read a book like this one. For God's sake, go to Jesus.

She was young and married. She had three children and a lot of responsibility. Nevertheless, she ran as far as she could go from her husband and family. She fled to another state and another life.

Her husband eventually found her and called. He said that he loved her and that the children loved her. But she had heard it all before. So she hung up.

Shortly thereafter, at great expense to himself—emotionally, physically, and financially—her husband traveled to her place of rebellion, loneliness, and pain. He begged her to come home . . . and she fell apart in his arms.

Later he asked her why, after he had begged on the phone and told her that he loved her, she had not returned. Her answer echoes every Christian who ever rebelled at the pain and ran from its source but who, nevertheless, returned home.

"Before it was only words," she answered. "Then you *came!*"

I move the previous question: What is God like?

By looking at Jesus, we discover two crucial facts about God that significantly impact our views on freedom and grace.

He Is Kind and He Is God

The oft-quoted comment of the beaver in C. S. Lewis's *The Lion, the Witch, and the Wardrobe* is on point. In the story Lucy asks the beaver if Aslan, the lion, is safe. The beaver says that the lion is, of course, not safe. Lions are never safe. Then the beaver insists that while Aslan isn't safe, he is good.[7]

If we can say no more about God than he is not safe, then, we are in for it. If God is the vindictive, angry, abusive deity that many tell us he is, then we have a serious problem. Given who we are, we can never please him. Nobody is that good, and nobody is that pure. We can, of course, sacrifice our firstborn; but even that won't be enough. We will live in constant fear, and with very good reason: "It is a fearful thing to fall into the hands of the living God."[8]

I have an acquaintance who writes me bunches of critical letters. In those letters, he always tells me that I disappoint God, "and after all he has done for you!" He reminds me that I'm too flippant, too joyful, too unorthodox, or too whatever. He always says to me, "How would you feel if Jesus came back today?" My friend has seen only one side of God. His God says, "Cry, will you? Cry, will you? OK, now I'll give you something to *really* cry about!"

Our teachers have threatened us that God is watching and that while we may get away with fooling people, we will never fool God. In the end the books will be balanced, and we will find ourselves in serious trouble. And so we cry.

On the other hand, are we in any better shape if God is kind, but also safe and controllable? I don't think so. In that case we have another problem. We have a god who isn't God at all.

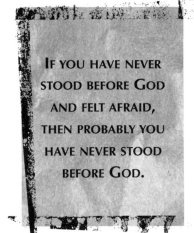

IF YOU HAVE NEVER STOOD BEFORE GOD AND FELT AFRAID, THEN PROBABLY YOU HAVE NEVER STOOD BEFORE GOD.

Little gods do little things. If you have never stood before God and felt afraid, then probably you have never stood before God. You have stood before an idol of your own making. Worse, your life will remain silly and superficial because you worship a silly and superficial god.

A number of evangelical theologians have recently tried to make god into their own image. They champion what is called Openness Theology. They deny that God is omniscient (or all knowing). "God can't know the future, nor does he know our choices, because the future hasn't yet happened and our future choices haven't yet been made," they say. I suppose they have good motives. I think they want to give us a postmodern god who seems quite rational, compassionate, and safe. Yet they do us a major disservice.

A user-friendly god is not God. That kind of god exists only in our imagination. He certainly is not the God of the Bible or the God who Jesus revealed to us.

At a recent meeting of the Evangelical Theological Society, a major debate took place on the subject of Openness Theology. The society voted some 70 percent to 30 percent that Openness Theology did not square with orthodox, biblical theology.

Frankly, I'm glad for that. I feel quite relieved. I'm sure that God feels relieved too. I'm sure he was saying to himself, "I hope I'm in charge . . . I was really worried there for a moment."

Silly? Of course it's silly. And God thinks so too. Listen to what he said to some ancient theologians who also tried to make him a bit more manageable: "You thought I was altogether like you. But I will rebuke you and accuse you to your face. Consider this, you who forget God, or I will tear you to pieces, with none to rescue."[9]

What we say about God has no bearing on who God really is. I can say that God is the Great Pumpkin, but my declaration doesn't make it so. God remains who he is.

I think it was C. S. Lewis who pointed out, in answer to Freud and others who charged that Christians had created and worshiped a "father" god out of their own desire, that we certainly wouldn't create the God revealed in the Bible. I know that if I created a god for myself, he would be far safer and far less terrifying than the one in the Bible.

God said through the prophet Isaiah, "For my thoughts are not your thoughts, neither are your ways my ways, declares the LORD. For as the heavens are higher than the earth, so are my ways higher than your ways and my thoughts than your thoughts."[10] Paul writes: "'For who has known the mind of the Lord, or who has been his counselor?' 'Or who has given a gift to him that he might be repaid?' For from him and through him and to him are all things. To him be glory forever. Amen."[11]

I can worship a God like that, a sovereign Lord both fully God and unimaginably kind. Those who bask in a "nice" Jesus and a "nice" God simply haven't read the Gospels. Even a cursory reading of the teaching and the actions of Jesus will reveal both the "kindness and sternness" of the real God (Romans 11:22).

Jesus talked about a "narrow way" that leads to life and a broad and easy one that leads to destruction. His anger at hypocrisy and religious manipulation knew no bounds. He taught clearly about God's judgment, hell, and the wrath of God. "The Son of Man will send his angels, and they will gather out of his kingdom all causes of sin and all law-breakers, and throw them into the fiery furnace. In that place there will be weeping and gnashing of teeth."[12] That, dear friend, is not a safe God.

At the same time, Jesus showed an incredible understanding of human weakness and sin. He hung around with winebibbers, sinners, and prostitutes. He ministered with gentleness and kindness to the broken. He said, "Come to me, all who labor and are heavy laden, and I will give you rest. Take my yoke upon you, and learn from me, for I am gentle and lowly in heart, and you will find rest for your souls. For my yoke is easy, and my burden is light."[13]

So is God confused? Quite the contrary! Only by understanding both the rule and the kindness of God do we find great personal balance and freedom.

A Bridge between Wrath and Love

Before we finish, we have to pause and consider the bridge between God's justified wrath and his amazing love. You know the verse by heart, but it helps to remember that "For God so loved the world, that he gave his only Son, that whoever believes in him should not perish but have eternal life. For God did not send his Son into the world to condemn the world, but in order that the world might be saved through him."[14]

The gospel is simple—simplicity on the other side of complexity.

We are needy, sinful, and helpless orphans birthed into a fallen world of darkness and death. God, out of his boundless compassion and love, has come himself and made us sons and daughters by the sacrifice of Christ. Aquinas rightly said that the cross did not secure the love of God, but the love of God secured the cross.

By trusting in Christ—and him alone—we become divine heirs. Orphans don't receive anything. The news is so phenomenally good that we can hardly stand it: "But to all who did receive him, who believed in his name, he gave the right to become children of God."[15] "For in Christ Jesus you are all sons of God, through faith."[16]

And not only did we get reconciled to a holy and righteous God through the sacrifice of Christ, something else happened: We received the righteousness of Christ. (We call the formal doctrine "imputed righteousness.") God transferred all the goodness of

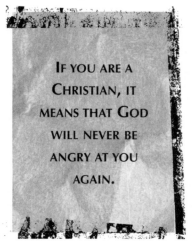

IF YOU ARE A CHRISTIAN, IT MEANS THAT GOD WILL NEVER BE ANGRY AT YOU AGAIN.

Christ to our account. "That is why his faith was 'counted to him as righteousness.' But the words 'it was counted to him' were not written for his sake alone, but for ours also. It [Christ's righteousness] will be counted ["imputed," KJV] to us who believe in him who raised from the dead Jesus our Lord, who was delivered up for our trespasses and raised for our justification."[17]

What does this mean? If you are a Christian, it means that God will never be angry at you again. God has turned away his wrath from you because he imputed (credited to your account) Christ's righteousness to you. And how can God be angry at perfection?

"There is therefore now no condemnation for those who are in Christ Jesus."[18] Paul expounds on the theme when he writes:

> Who shall bring any charge against God's elect? It is God who justifies. Who is to condemn? Christ Jesus is the one who died—more than that, who was raised—who is at the right hand of God, who indeed is interceding for us. Who shall separate us from the love of Christ? Shall tribulation, or distress, or persecution, or famine, or nakedness, or danger, or sword? . . . No in all these things we are more than conquerors through him who loved us. For I am sure that neither death nor life, nor angels nor rulers, nor things present nor things to come, nor powers, nor height nor depth, nor anything else in all creation, will be able to separate us from the love of God in Christ Jesus our Lord.[19]

God is God and God is not safe. In fact, he's kind of scary.

I'm glad.

God is also good, kind, and compassionate. I'm glad about that too.

God isn't angry. And that's a downright relief.

Now, may I ask a question? If you really, *really* believed that God was good (not safe, but good), that he was in charge of this mess, and that he never grew angry with you—how would you act? What would you do? How would you order your life? What kinds of things would you change?

Jesus said, "So if the Son sets you free, you will be free indeed."[20]

DON'T YOU WISH YOU DID?

A friend of mine pastored a church near a major English university. Eager to make an impact, his church held a wine-and-cheese-tasting party (they do it differently in England) and invited the university's entire theological faculty to attend.

One professor, a liberal woman who had long since given up her "childish" views of God, got a bit tipsy. She leaned over to my pastor friend, who earlier that evening had expressed his orthodox views about God, and said, "You know, I don't believe that stuff is true."

"I know," my friend replied, "but don't you wish you did?"

This is a book about freedom, but it is really more a book about God—not about a god we have created from our guilt and our neurotic need for punishment, but about the real God who would have us laugh, sing, and dance. In his book *Practicing the Presence of People*, Mike Mason writes:

> How much freedom do you want? Do you want to be completely free of shame and guilt and know that you are respected, cherished, and loved without limit? Do you want to be free to be fully, outrageously yourself? Do you want to be exactly who you are, no strings attached? . . .
>
> If this is what you want, then begin by setting your God free. Don't condemn the awesome King of the universe to a dull existence in a box. Let God be God, and He'll let you be you.[21]

Mason's comments remind me of a convent school where a basket of apples sat on the dining-room table. A note under the basket said, "Take only one. God is watching."

At the other end of the dining room sat another basket filled with chocolate-chip cookies. In a child's handwriting, a note under the basket read: "Take all the cookies you want. God is watching the apples."

If you don't have time to read the rest of this book, let me sum it up. God really is watching both the apples and the cookies. In fact, he made them for you and will be offended if you don't try them.

He may even enjoy a few himself.

For I know that nothing good dwells in me, that is, in my flesh. For I have the desire to do what is right, but not the ability to carry it out.

—Romans 7:18

CHAPTER
THREE

THE PERFECTION WE DESIRE...
and the Forgiveness That Sets Us Free

HUMAN EXCELLENCE, APART FROM GOD, IS LIKE THE FABLED
FLOWER WHICH, ACCORDING TO THE RABBIS, EVE PLUCKED
WHEN PASSING OUT OF PARADISE. SEVERED FROM ITS NATIVE
ROOT, IT IS ONLY THE TOUCHING MEMORIAL OF A LOST EDEN—
SAD WHILE CHARMING AND BEAUTIFUL, BUT DEAD.
—SIR CHARLES VILLIERS STANFORD

I have a confession to make. But before I make it, I must give you an idea of where I'm going.

Now that I have your attention, let me ask you a question: Are you getting much better than you were? In other words, with all of the teaching you've received about obedience, holiness, and sanctification, is it working in your life? I know, at the beginning of your walk with Christ, you saw some major changes for the good—but after that, did you get much better?

If you are a reasonably good citizen, fairly active in the church, don't do the "big" sins (at least, publicly), and try really hard, you probably have to admit, if you're honest with yourself, that you aren't getting much better. You probably feel the weight of conviction much of the time and wince when the preacher gets too close to home. I suspect that you really want to be better. I'll bet you wish you could love your wife/husband more, be a better mother/father, become more compassionate and kind, be more committed to Christ and his work, more faithfully share your faith, give more to missions or go yourself, care more for the poor, be a better witness . . . and the list goes on and on.

In his great book *Holiness by Grace*, Bryan Chapell tells about Walter Marshall, the seventeenth-century pastor and author of *The Gospel Mystery of Sanctification*, who said to his congregation, "May God bless my discovery of the powerful means of holiness so far as to save some from killing themselves."[1]

The people in Marshall's church were literally killing themselves in their efforts to be godly. They practiced self-mutilation, deprivation, and inflicted all kinds of pain on themselves in efforts to please God and be pure. Few of us go that far—we have television, movies, and parties to divert our attention from our guilt. Nevertheless, we know that we aren't getting much better, and it drives many of us into denial or out of the church.

I have a friend who was disciplined by a Bible college he attended. He and some friends left campus one evening, visited a local bar, and got drunk. When he was caught, the college administration decided to shun him. All of the students were required to turn their backs on him when he walked by and to have nothing to do with him.

"Steve," he told me, "I understood the discipline and even knew I deserved it. The thing that bothered me was that those who got drunk with me, but were never caught, shunned me too." My friend left the college and almost left the Christian faith.

I suspect we have all been admonished, preached to, judged, corrected, and disciplined by people who were committing the same sins that haunted us. In their efforts to make us feel guilty, they were simply diverting attention from themselves.

Some people find it very easy to manipulate others. They know that most people aren't getting much better, and it is a short step from that knowledge to manipulation. Power and self-righteousness can be wonderfully addictive and easily acquired by accusing others. Believe me, I know; I'm an expert.

When Paul talks about the abolition of the law in the book of Romans, he gives us a powerful way to get better, because he knew that getting better wasn't the point. Our relationship with God is the point, and that is the place where we ought to get obsessive. When I am obsessed with being better instead of being consumed with God's love and grace, I become prideful if I can pull it off and self-centered if I can't.

The greatest cause for our not getting better is our obsession with not getting better. There is a better way of getting better than trying harder. Sanctification becomes a reality in those believers who don't obsess over their own sanctification. Holiness hardly ever becomes a reality until we care more about Jesus than about holiness.

But I'm getting ahead of myself.

TIRED OF TRYING

Now let me give you my confession: I'm about as good as I'm going to get, and I'm tired of trying. I know we've all been taught that Christians are supposed to get better and better every day and in every way. But I've been trying for a long time, and it just isn't working.

I once thought if I could just stop smoking my pipe, I would be perfect. But then God showed me some other bad stuff in my life. From that time on, I've been trying to deal with what he showed me, and after all my efforts, it still isn't working.

When I realized I wasn't going to get much better, I thought I would feel depressed. Everybody told me that I needed to be better. Some told me that I could reach a point where I would have no known sin in my life. When I was ordained, the bishop used the words of John Wesley to ask me if I were moving on to perfection. I said that I was, and I thought I spoke truth. It was a big dream.

When I became acutely aware that perfection wasn't going to be realized (at least, not all of the time), I prepared myself for the inevitable despondency that follows the death of a dream. At first I thought I wouldn't tell people that I wasn't going to get a whole lot better. After all, a lot of people look up to me as a Christian leader— being on the radio and all—and I wouldn't want to hurt them. Then there was my mother, who thought I was close to perfect anyway. I

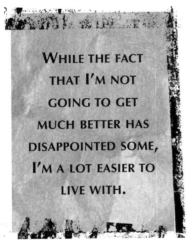

WHILE THE FACT THAT I'M NOT GOING TO GET MUCH BETTER HAS DISAPPOINTED SOME, I'M A LOT EASIER TO LIVE WITH.

didn't want to tell her because I didn't want to dash her high hopes. At the time I realized the truth, I was a pastor and certainly wasn't going to tell the people in my church. They would be so very disappointed, maybe even angry.

So, for a long time, I faked it. While I'm not good at the perfection thing, I'm quite good at faking it. A friend of mine once told me that Christians appear to be better than everyone else because we know the rules and can fake it better than non-Christians can. He was right.

I know what's running through your mind. You're thinking of all kinds of things I need to do. You're thinking that I need to be in the Word more often, I need to pray more, and I certainly need to be in an accountable relationship.

Just so you know, I'm a Bible teacher and spend much of my day in the Word. I am a man of prayer and have written a book on prayer. And I'm in at least two accountability groups.

But I'm still not going to get much better than I am.

As I mentioned, I thought I would be depressed when I finally came out of the closet and told people I wasn't going to get much better. But, in fact, I didn't get depressed. My wife didn't leave, and my children didn't disown me. (My family told me later that they had realized long before I did that I wasn't getting a whole lot better.) The church didn't fire me, and my friends who loved me didn't get angry. And best of all, God loved me anyway.

There is hardly anything that will beat you down and rob you of your freedom more than *your* efforts to get better—or, at least, the effort to get better in the wrong way. C. S. Lewis, in writing about people trying to live by the law of God, said:

> Either we give up trying to be good, or else we become very unhappy indeed. For, make no mistake: If you are really going to try to meet all the demands made on the natural self, it will not have enough left over to live on. The more you obey your conscience, the more your conscience will demand of you. And your natural self, which is thus being starved and hampered and worried at every turn, will get angrier. In the end, you will either give up trying to be good, or else become one of those people who, as they say, "live for others" but always in a discontented, grumbling way—always making a martyr of yourself. And once you have become that you will be a far greater pest to anyone who has to live with you than you would have been if you had remained frankly selfish.[2]

While the fact that I'm not going to get much better has disappointed some, I'm a lot easier to live with. I even have some friends now whom I didn't have before. I couldn't associate with them when I thought I was getting better. You know . . . bad company ruins good morals. Besides, when I was faking it, I couldn't let people get too close. They might find out the truth, and I was trying so very hard to keep the truth from them.

You may be thinking that I care nothing for the law of God, for his plan for me, and for my own sanctification. But stay with me. I have some surprising information to share with you.

AGAINST THE LAW?

Antinomian is a word (coined by Martin Luther) that literally means "against the law." Antinomianism is the view that the will of God in our lives, as expressed in the Bible, is irrelevant and no longer a part of God's call on the life of the believer.

Paul addressed the problem of antinomianism when he wrote: "What shall we say then? Are we to continue in sin that grace may abound? By no means! How can we who died to sin still live in it? . . . What then? Are we to sin because we are not under law but under grace? By no means!"[3] While perfectionism considerably inhibits our freedom, so does antinomianism.

The psalmist praises God's revelation of his will for us: "But you are near, O LORD, and all your commandments are true. Long have I known from your testimonies that you have founded them forever."[4] "Oh how I love your law! It is my meditation all the day. Your commandment makes me wiser than my enemies."[5] Paul writes that the law of God is our teacher before we come to Christ[6] and, by implication, continues in that role throughout our lives. Any view suggesting that God no longer has any concern for our obedience to him and his ways is sheer nonsense.

Whether or not I can be obedient—be any better than I am—is irrelevant to the fact that God has some strong views on right and wrong, good and evil, moral and immoral. Because he is God, his views are not opinions; they are, in fact, a revelation about what is right and wrong, good and evil, moral and immoral. We don't like it much, but we don't get a vote; and if you think about it for a moment, you wouldn't have it any other way.

Let me once again give you the principle I offered in chapter 2: *If*

there is no God, there are no values; if there are no values, there is no mean-
ing; and if there is no meaning, you are a turnip and will simply live for a
while, die, and then go back to the soil from which you came.

I may not be a good person, but I know that goodness in itself is
a good thing for me and for the society in which I live. I may not be
able to love, but I know that loving is better than hating. I may not
be always honest, but I know that honesty is a good thing and better
than dishonesty.

The late Walter Martin, the founder of the Christian Research
Institute, once appeared on a talk show in New York. The other
guest, a Jewish atheist, asserted that all values were relevant only to
the society that shared those values. In other words, we sort of vote
on what we want to be good or evil, and while those views may be
helpful for my particular society, they can't be made into universal
laws of good and evil.

Martin, who held a Ph.D., said that if time had allowed, he could
have gone down a complicated and intricate philosophical road to
prove the other guest wrong. But Walter knew he had to make his
point quickly and simply. So he said to the Jewish atheist: "Let's
play a game of pretend."

"OK," replied the guest.

"Let's pretend," said Martin, "that we are living in the Third
Reich and I'm a member of the SS. Further, let's pretend that I and
the others with me have just rousted you out of your bed, taken you
to SS headquarters, and I now have a German Luger pointed at your
head. You tell me why I shouldn't pull the trigger."

All of a sudden, Martin said, it wasn't a game. What had begun
as a pretend exercise took on existential meaning.

"You can't do that!" the atheist replied.

"Why not?" asked Martin.

"Because it's wrong."

"No, it isn't wrong. You just said that all values are relevant only to the society in which they are found. We, as a society, have declared that you are a member of an inferior race and have decided to rid ourselves of you and those like you. Why is it wrong?"

Of course, Martin won the argument, because even the most avid postmodernist who disavows any absolute value simply can't live that way. Certain standards really are absolute. All of us know (even if we deny it) that love is better than hate, honesty is better than dishonesty, and faithfulness is better than unfaithfulness. Atheists violate their own philosophy in the living of their lives—unless, of course, they become totally selfish and evil. In fact, much of atheism is a desire for autonomy from a sovereign God.

That is why they shout so loud and protest so much.

The point is this: When we say that we aren't going to get much better, we don't mean that "getting better" isn't a good thing. In fact, just the opposite. We want to be better people than we are because . . . well . . . because we know that being better is better.

God isn't a spoilsport. He doesn't find out what we enjoy and then take delight in telling us that it is wrong and that, if we don't get in line, he will punish us. As we have seen, some define sin as what you enjoy, and if you didn't enjoy it, it wasn't sin.

Nothing could be further from the truth. God's laws are his gift to us. They reflect the way the world works. If you want to know the best way to live, live according to God's instructions. If you want to be reasonably happy, live according to the instructions God has given. If you want to be reasonably healthy and wise, then do what God says. God doesn't tell us adultery is wrong because he thinks sex is nasty. He tells us that adultery is wrong because it can destroy your life, the life of your spouse, and the lives of your children. He doesn't tell us to forgive to keep us from getting justice. He says to forgive because it's the best thing for your heart and your stomach. Bitterness, in the end, will destroy you and rob you of your peace.

Yesterday I listened to a local talk-show host interview a woman who had forgiven the murderer of her husband. She had even pleaded with the court not to execute the killer. Further, after the execution of the man, she visited his grave in order to find closure in terms of her forgiveness. The talk-show host called the woman crazy and said that, if someone killed him, he wouldn't want his wife visiting the grave of his killer, "unless she does it to spit on his grave."

Then this host asked his listeners to call and comment. One man said, "I don't know if I could visit the grave and forgive the person who killed my spouse, but I wish I could, because I know that bitterness could hurt me terribly." He understood. Common sense seems to require both justice and revenge. But something in that man's heart nudged him toward forgiveness, even as something necessary.

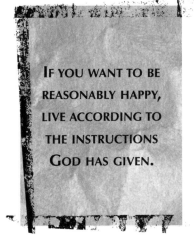

IF YOU WANT TO BE REASONABLY HAPPY, LIVE ACCORDING TO THE INSTRUCTIONS GOD HAS GIVEN.

During my many years as a pastor, I listened to more confessions than a district attorney prosecuting a political fund-raising scandal. Without exception, I saw regret and sorrow. I heard one sentence more than any other: "If only I could do it again." I, too, have often used that sentence. I know about the valley of regret because I've been there many times.

SHOULD I KEEP TRYING?

You may have a few questions at this point: "If being better is a good thing, then would it not also be a good thing to keep on trying? Isn't it better to have a goal and miss it than to have no goal at all? If I have a goal to be better or even perfect, won't I come closer to perfection than I would if I had no goal?"

Good point.

Actually, there is a sense in which our quest for perfection is an indication—albeit in a negative and debilitating way—of something good. The downside is that if you don't watch it, it will rob you of your freedom. But the upside is something good.

When I said I didn't think I was going to get much better, the operative word there is "I," not "getting better." When I said I was giving up, I was talking about my own self-powered efforts at getting better. When I gave up, I think I finally understood Paul's problem when he said he wanted to do good, but when he tried, he did the very thing he didn't want to do (Romans 7). When I gave up, I gave up on me and my obsession.

The focus of my teaching is grace. I keep that focus because I so desperately need grace. In our broadcast, in my teaching, and in my books, I tell God's people that, because of Christ, God isn't angry at them and never will be angry at them. Some say, however, that I am encouraging sin by my teaching.

V. Raymond Edman, the former president of Wheaton College, used to say, "We don't encourage dating at Wheaton . . . we don't have to!" Well, I don't encourage sin in what I teach—I don't have to! Christians do fine in the sin area without any encouragement. I don't think I've ever met a Christian man or woman who didn't *want* to be better than he or she was. They were just going about it the wrong way . . . trying really hard to be better.

A GOOD THING IN A STRANGE WAY

Despite what I've said, trying to be perfect has been a very good thing for me. At first it took away my freedom, but then it gave it back. Do you know why?

Because if I hadn't tried, I wouldn't have known I couldn't do it. If I hadn't tried, I would wonder if my lack of effort pointed to a problem far more serious than the fact that I couldn't get better. It's one thing to do wrong and to know that what I'm doing is wrong. It is quite another to do wrong and not to know it is wrong.

If you had never desired to be better than you are, it is a good indication that something is missing in your heart. As I understand it, the Holy Spirit gives the desire, and the presence of that desire is a sure sign of the Spirit. Jesus said,

> If you love me, you will keep my commandments. And I will ask the Father, and he will give you another Helper, to be with you forever, even the Spirit of truth, whom the world cannot receive, because it neither sees him nor knows him. You know him, for he dwells with you and will be in you. I will not leave you as orphans; I will come to you.[7]

The very fact that you want to be better—even perfect—is a sign that you belong to Christ. One of the best ways to find assurance of your salvation is not so much to examine what you do, but to look carefully at what you *want* to do.

I was a pastor long before I was a Christian (or, at least, before I was a *red hot* one). I've always had a glib tongue, and the church required that I talk each Sunday morning. No problem. And then the job required that I be nice, visit hospitals on occasion, and look reasonably spiritual. I could do that too. And then, after I had done all that, I was free to fish and play golf. I thought I had died and gone to heaven. I thought, *Is this a great job or what?*

That is when Jesus came and messed up a very good thing. He began to teach me that his job description was very different from mine. He put the people on my heart and caused me to love them. He gave me the Bible as a source of authority and commissioned me to teach others about what I had found therein. He showed me his love, and because of that love, I wanted desperately to please him.

I blew it a lot. I made a lot of mistakes. I sometimes wish I could go back to that little church I served on Cape Cod and correct some of those mistakes. When Jesus came, however, I wanted desperately to please him. *And in that wanting, I found confirmation of God's call to be their pastor.*

The desire for perfection indicates the presence in us of *something* or *someone* who has given us that desire. That someone is the Holy

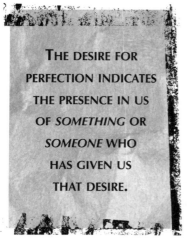

THE DESIRE FOR PERFECTION INDICATES THE PRESENCE IN US OF *SOMETHING* OR *SOMEONE* WHO HAS GIVEN US THAT DESIRE.

Spirit; we feel his presence in the desire. It is also the Holy Spirit who brings us to the point of simply giving up that which we can't do anyway.

I have a dear friend who, in the last two or three years, has come close to tears whenever we talk about certain important matters. I'm a fixer, and fixers, when they see tears, see a problem that needs to be fixed. I offered all kinds of suggestions to my friend to stop the tears and to make her feel better. Finally, after a number of failed attempts, she said to me, "Stop it! Just stop it. My tears are good."

When I asked my friend to please explain herself, she told me that for many years she felt separate from her own pain and the pain of others. "I was," she said, "compassionate in a way. I cared about what people were going through—but there was this barrier that kept me from really feeling the things that hurt them. I even separated myself from my own pain." Then my friend said something profound. "Steve," she said, "my tears are good because they let me know I'm real."

It's the same way with our salvation. If we just don't give a flip, we probably don't know the Lord at all; but in the caring, we find confirmation that our concern came from him. When we desire perfection and when we desire to be better than we are, God confirms in our hearts that we belong to him.

THE CREATION OF A MONSTER

Unfortunately, that desire to be better can become something else—a "monster" that robs you of your freedom. The downside of the desire to be better is perfectionism.

Perfectionism is the belief that one can be perfect—or at least better than everybody else. Perfectionism will make you sour, mean, and judgmental, and it will rob you of the freedom Jesus died to give you. Not only will it rob you of your freedom, it will make you a horrible bore.

Beware the Freedom Robber

It's not very smart to keep trying to do something you can't do and never will be able to do. So consider the first plague of perfectionism: *Perfectionism robs you of your freedom.*

That is why I gave up. When Paul honestly admitted his inability to do the good he wanted to do, he took the first step in the direction of health. With astounding honesty, Paul wrote, "I do not understand my own actions. For I do not do what I want, but I do the very thing I hate. . . . For I do not do the good I want, but the evil I do not want is what I keep on doing."[8]

When I read those words, I think, *Paul, I don't believe I would have said that. What will people think?* But then I realize what a major relief and what freedom it must have brought to Paul to finally face the reality of his own helplessness and hopelessness.

Have you ever come to that point? If you're still trying to be perfect—despite plenteous evidence to suggest that you are never going to get there—you are doing something quite foolish and destructive to your freedom.

Do you remember Sisyphus? In Greek mythology, he was the son of Aeolus and the founder of Ephyre. He revealed Zeus's rape of Aegina to her father, and as his punishment, Zeus doomed him for all of eternity to roll a huge stone up a hill, only to have it roll down again each time.

Perfectionist, thy name is Sisyphus!

Aren't you tired of it? Isn't that huge stone getting to be a bore? Don't you wish you could just leave the stupid stone at the bottom of the hill and walk away? Aren't you tired of trying and trying, yet never getting much better? Me too. That's why I've given up—and I have found such great relief and freedom in giving up.

Beware the Curse of Pretending

Certain kinds of pretending can kill you. That's the second thing about perfectionism that you need to know. Let me say it like this: *You greatly diminish your freedom when you pretend to others that you are accomplishing perfection.*

Before I gave up, I spent half of my time trying to do something I couldn't do and the other half of my time trying to convince others that I had done it. It is called hypocrisy, and it is quite human and quite injurious to your sanity . . . as well as your freedom. That's why I gave it up.

One of my problems is that I like to be liked. I spend most of my social and professional life around Christians, so it is mostly Christians I want to please. Any "real" Christian must say and do certain things, thus ensuring acceptance by the Christian community. You have to subscribe to a certain standard and live reasonably close to it; you must use certain catchwords popular in the Christian community; and you must never express doubts or ask questions.

Among the "biggies" of being a "real" Christian, for instance, is how one feels about those who don't know Christ. If you are a Christian, you should be terribly concerned about the lost of the world. While I always said I felt concerned about them, the problem was that I didn't even know their names. Don't misunderstand! I am faithful in my witness to the lost; I teach and practice evangelism; and I consider the command of Christ to make disciples an absolute. Jesus didn't request; he commanded. And I am, after all, his servant.

But no matter how hard I tried, I just couldn't muster much compassion for the lost. I had friends who can stand in a mall and literally weep for the lost as they walk by. Their genuine concern intimidated me, and knowing that a "real" Christian must have a broken heart for the lost, I tried to appear to be in as much pain as possible. I can't fake tears, but I do pretty well with the serious and sad-countenance thing.

Now, don't get me wrong. I care very much for those I know and love. If I have a friend or a family member who doesn't know Christ, I will do everything possible to share my faith with him or her in a way that will bring that person into the kingdom. In fact, I suspect a number of friends have become Christians just to shut me up. However (and I'm not proud of this and have asked God to change it), I just don't care about the teeming masses.

I thought I was the only one who felt like this until, while meeting with a group of Christians, I had an attack of insanity and confessed it. One would have thought that I had burped at a funeral. Everybody got very quiet. I prepared myself for the inevitable criticism.

But do you know what happened?

"You too?" one man said quietly. "I thought I was the only one."

"I feel that way too," said someone else, "and I've always felt guilty about it."

"You're the first person I ever heard admit that. That's sad, but it is refreshing. I've felt that way, too, but thought that you guys would reject me if I told you."

One after another, my friends confessed they had trouble mustering up compassion for people they didn't know. Now we're praying for one another about our desire to care. I'm not there yet, but I'm better than I was. And who knows? I might find one day that I stand in malls and weep over the lost. But whether or not that happens, I sleep better. It takes a lot of emotional "gasoline" to fake compassion. Besides, when you keep on faking it, it's hard to know when you have the real thing.

Do you have doubts? So does everyone else.

Do you have a secret that, if your friends knew, you would be so ashamed that you might even get suicidal? Welcome to the club.

Do you sometimes commit "first degree" sin? Me too. (What is it about us that requires us to tell our friends that we didn't mean to sin, that it sort of sneaked up on us, and before we knew it, we were done for? Frankly, most of the sin I've committed has been first degree—I thought about it before I did it. Sometimes I thought about it for a long time.)

Do you have trouble forgiving people for the way they have devalued you? You might be surprised at the number of Christians who have trouble with that.

Do some Christians just drive you up a wall, to say nothing about pagans? They give me problems sometimes too.

Do you sometimes get angry without reason and say things that cause you to blush later? Sometimes I get so angry that, when I spit, the grass withers.

Do you ever try really hard to be good, kind, and loving, only to reach the conclusion that it just isn't "doable"? I understand.

Do you struggle with paranoia? Me too. And sometimes, even knowing that I'm paranoid, I still think they are after me.

Do you sometimes think that if people really knew you, they wouldn't like you and, in fact, would think you weren't a Christian? You too?

Dr. Reggie Kidd is one of my colleagues at the seminary where I teach. He is one of the finest scholars I know, as well as one of the most free and most vulnerable people I know. We team teach a course called Theology of Ministry.

During one class I lectured on "The Seven Deadly Sins of the Pastor," using the ancient monastic description of sin as my jumping-off place. The seven deadly sins go back, at least, to Pope Saint Gregory the Great and Saint John Cassian. The Bible addresses all of these sins. There are seven corre-sponding virtues. Reggie lectures on those; it is a correct assignment, given my sin and his goodness.

IT TAKES A LOT OF EMOTIONAL "GASOLINE" TO FAKE COMPASSION.

After the three-hour lecture, Reggie asked me during the break, "Steve, are you going to unpack that a bit more?" I told him that I had said all I was going to say, but he was welcome to address the group.

Do you know what he did? He stood before a class of theological students and began to go down the list of deadly sins, confessing his personal sins in each area. He literally "took off his armor." As I sat in the back of that class, I remember thinking, *Man, he has courage.*

When Reggie finished, nobody moved. You could have heard a pin drop, and I thought I heard an angel sing. I spoke into the silence of the classroom: "Do you folks know the gift you have been given? It is one you should value the rest of your lives. One of the most godly and respected men I know just confessed his sin before you so that you might be free, loved, and understand grace. Be very thankful."

After the class I don't think I've ever seen such joy and freedom in any seminary classroom. The students surrounded Reggie, patted him on the back, and thanked him. Then a group of the students took him out to lunch.

Are you a sinner? Me too! You probably already knew that. But let me tell you something else: So is everyone else . . . Martin Luther, John Wesley, Billy Graham, Mother Teresa, and your pastor. None of us is probably going to get a whole lot better—and yet Jesus is still fond of us.

There, now, don't you feel better? I know. I know. You also feel guilty. That brings me to the third thing about perfectionism that affects your freedom.

Beware the Wrong Road

It is not only crazy to keep trying to do the impossible and to convince others that you have done the impossible, *it is also crazy to keep going down the wrong road, thinking that your speed and length of travel will turn the wrong road into the right road.*

Edison, after he had tried and failed thousands of times to find a filament that would make his light bulb possible, responded to someone who said he was wasting his time. "No, it wasn't a waste of my time. Now I know ten thousand ways *not* to do it."

The problem with trying to do something you can't do, and the problem with pretending to others you have done it, isn't just that it's stupid; it also wastes time and effort that you could devote to something more productive, such as . . . playing golf, reading, going to a movie, talking with friends, or maybe even praying.

WHO REALLY GETS BETTER?

Let me share with you a major biblical principle and the only reason I've given up trying to be better: *The only people who get better are*

people who know that, if they never get better, God will love them anyway.
The corollary to that principle is this: *God will not only love you if you*
don't get better; he will teach you that getting better isn't the issue. His
love is the issue.

Out of the love, kindness, and presence of God, you will find
yourself getting better.

On August 21, 1544, Martin Luther wrote a letter to George
Spalatin, a Christian brother who had worked with Luther in the
Reformation. Spalatin was suffering terribly from enormous guilt
about some spurious advice he had given. He was devastated, guilt
ridden, and depressed. Luther, learning of his condition, wrote to
him the following:

> My faithful request and admonition is that you join our company
> and associate with us, who are real, great, and hardboiled sinners.
>
> You must by no means make Christ to seem paltry and trifling
> to us, as though He could be our Helper only when we want to be
> rid from imaginary, nominal, and childish sins. No, no! That
> would not be good for us.
>
> He must rather be a Savior and Redeemer from real, great,
> grievous and damnable transgressions and iniquities, yea, from
> the very greatest and most shocking sins; to be brief, from all sins
> added together in a grand total.[9]

How often have we Christians, not unlike Luther's friend, spent
wasted hours of remorse over our lack of perfection or pretending
that we have more of it than we have?

If that were all there was to it, it would simply be neurotic. Our
honest belief that we can be far better than we are is one of the major
reasons we are so bound. Our freedom has been taken away
because we thought that we couldn't be free unless we were perfect.

Guilt has only one purpose: to drive us to the throne of grace,
where we allow God, if he deems to do so, to change us and make
us better. When we allow guilt to do anything other than that, we

become perfectionists—miserable, dishonest, guilt ridden, afraid, and lonely.

Miserable because of the hopelessness of the task. *Dishonest* because there is no way we can be as perfect as we want others to think we are. *Guilt ridden* because we have this false belief that God, aside from Christ's righteousness given to us, expects perfection. *Afraid* because we don't want others to know how bad we really are. And *lonely* because perfectionists are a pain in the neck.

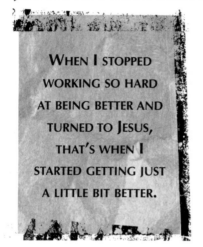

WHEN I STOPPED WORKING SO HARD AT BEING BETTER AND TURNED TO JESUS, THAT'S WHEN I STARTED GETTING JUST A LITTLE BIT BETTER.

Has someone ever come to you, asking for forgiveness, when you didn't even know there was need for forgiveness? A man did that to me the other day. "Steve," he said, "I'm so sorry for what I've been thinking about you. I've been unfair and un-Christian in what I've thought about you and what I've said to others. Can you find it in your heart to forgive me?"

I, of course, forgave him. I barely knew him, and it was easy to forgive . . . at first.

But then I started thinking about what he said. I wondered what he had been thinking. Did he think that I was a hypocrite? Did he think that I was a heretic, a failure, arrogant, rude, and superficial? And what in the world had he been saying to others? My reputation is important, and perhaps he was trying to ruin it. In fact, my whole ministry could be brought down because of what he said. He might have been talking to colleagues or friends.

Then my paranoia kicked in, and I wondered why some of my friends hadn't called lately, why the president of the seminary had seemed to be avoiding me, and why my pastor, during the sermon, seemed to look at me more than others. Then I thought, *You know, I bet that turkey wasn't even sincere when he asked for forgiveness. He knew what I would think, and he was trying to get me.*

If I could have remembered the man's name, I would have told him I thought he was a twit, that I didn't forgive him, and that I didn't appreciate what he'd been thinking and saying about me.

You're right, that's neurotic. He was just as neurotic, though, when he asked me to forgive him for something that, as far as I was concerned, didn't need forgiving.

God doesn't dwell on our sins the way I did. God doesn't wonder what we've been saying about him, and he doesn't think we might not be sincere or genuinely repentant. In what that man said to me, however, there is a bit of how we go to God, trying to keep him from being angry and begging him to forgive us.

There really is something neurotic about Christians who spend most of their time trying desperately to please a God who is already very pleased. They don't have any freedom, and they sometimes take away the freedom of others.

I noticed the other day that I'm beginning to look a little like Jesus. I'm loving a bit more the way he loves. I care for people more like Jesus cares for people. I'm a tad more obedient, more like how Jesus was obedient. I do think I'm getting better.

But that isn't the point. Jesus is the point.

I'm getting better by not trying so hard to be better. Almost everything of any importance (love, happiness, contentment) comes when I am looking for something else. When I stopped working so hard at being better and turned to Jesus, that's when, almost without noticing it, I started getting just a little bit better. So I have decided to get as close as I can to Jesus, who will always love me even if I don't get any better.

Radio listeners, however, are another matter.

AM I *REALLY* GETTING BETTER?

I got a letter from an upset listener last week. He was upset with me because I had quoted 1 Corinthians 10:12: "Therefore let anyone who thinks that he stands take heed lest he fall." I'd said that the most dangerous thing in the lives of Christians is their obedience when they know they are being obedient, and that the best gift we have is our sin when we know we are sinning. The listener quoted a lot of Scripture, and I had decided he was right. In fact, I decided to make a correction on the broadcast and repent in sackcloth and ashes . . . publicly.

And I hate doing that.

But then God whispered to me: *You really are getting better.*

I protested that it didn't *feel* like I was getting better. But as God spoke to my heart, I began to understand that if I felt like I was getting much better, my proclivity for self-righteousness would drive me to tell everybody; and while I am getting better, I still have a very long way to go. The closer I am to God, the more I see the truth about myself and how very far off the destination really is.

When I first met God, I told him that I would always be obedient, always serve him faithfully, and always be pure and good. God must have lovingly laughed at my naiveté. But as I have walked with him over these years, he's shown me things I didn't even know were a part of me. His light does that to darkness.

So, the truth of the matter is, I'm better because I'm closer to him; but the closer I am to him, the less I *feel* I'm getting better. It may sound crazy, but it's true. If I knew I was getting better, I would feel quite self-sufficient; and before I knew it, I would be offering to help God out a bit, then I would start helping others get better the way I did.

But in reality, making others better is God's job, not mine.

God chose to be my friend not to make me better but because he wanted to be my friend. Rather than obsessing about my goodness, God asks me to hang out with him and see where he leads me. He promises that he will never leave me or forsake me. So I can quit worrying about getting behind in my holiness and sanctification. The more I worry about that, the worse I'm going to get, but the more I abide with him, the better I'll get—even if I don't know it.

In Philippians 1:6 Paul says that what God begins, he brings to completion. That means God's beginning in our lives is the absolute promise that he will continue working to completion.

So I know I'm better than I was. Wish I could tell you how I got better, but God won't tell me; and most of the time, he won't tell you either. We're just going to have to trust the Spirit in each of us that God is making us like his Son . . . even if it isn't the picture they gave us in Sunday school.

That's a long way around the barn to speak an important truth: The most godly person you know is not the one you thought. Not only that. The most godly person you know probably doesn't even know that he or she is altogether that godly.

FOR ALL THE PROMISES OF GOD FIND
THEIR YES IN HIM. THAT IS WHY IT IS THROUGH HIM
THAT WE UTTER OUR
AMEN TO GOD FOR HIS GLORY.
—2 CORINTHIANS 1:20

CHAPTER
FOUR
THE GOSPEL WE FORGET ...
and the Joy That Sets Us Free

JOY TO THE WORLD! THE LORD IS COME;
LET EARTH RECEIVE HER KING.
—ISAAC WATTS; PSALM 98

"The church is a prostitute," Augustine said, "but she is my mother."

If you don't understand what he meant, you need to read this chapter, because sometimes religious institutions can kill off your freedom and your joy.

A HARD TASKMASTER

Let me say something that might surprise you. I hate religion. I just hate it! Religion is probably necessary, and it's a fact of life. Religions and religious people, like weeds, are everywhere, and you can't get rid of them. Something innate in us seems to require religious expression; and all expression, by nature, eventually becomes institutionalized. The institution of religion can be a very hard taskmaster and can demand your soul by putting you in a prison of guilt and shame. And only God has the right to demand your soul.

Now I have to be careful here. Anything I say should be seen in the context of my love for the church. I'm so glad that I'm a part of Christ's visible church—but sometimes, church looks more like a prison than it does a gateway to freedom.

I've been a religious professional for most of my life. I have—and this is a confession—been (and still am, I fear) a participant in and a leader of what we all know, in our saner moments, to be something less than a healthy religious system.

Religion can make people mean, angry, gloomy, critical, judgmental, and neurotic. Religion can also become an abuser of Christians. I have seen so many people hurt by religion that I sometimes think it would be better to be a pagan.

Worst of all, religion can keep you from God. It can become the substitute—and not a very good one—for a relationship with God himself. Something about institutional Christianity (as necessary as it is) will kill your freedom, if you aren't careful.

Whenever a new Christian comes into the church, I wince a bit, because I'm afraid that they will get the "religion disease," that the "church virus" will kill off the joy and freedom Jesus purchased on the cross to give them.

DOWN THE WRONG ROAD

Have you ever watched new Christians go down the road of getting "religionized"? It starts with a genuine discovery that there is a God, that he is love, and that he has forgiven them and accepted them. I find it so refreshing when new Christians discover the words of Paul in 2 Corinthians 5:19—"In Christ God was reconciling the world to himself, not counting their trespasses against them—and that the saying is trustworthy and deserving of full acceptance, that Christ Jesus came into the world to save sinners, of whom I am the foremost."[1]

That is, until religion gets hold of them.

Then the new Christians hear of a whole morass of "stuff" they need to learn. They must learn who is right and who is wrong—who the good guys and the bad guys are—with the requirement that new Christians choose sides in the us-and-them battle. They must learn the "correct" version of the Bible, the "correct" behavior for a Christian, and the "correct" political position they should take on a variety of issues. Then, as new Christians get discipled, they learn about the "correct" and Christian way to rear a family, conduct a business, and discipline one's life so the world will feel drawn to Christ.

Did you hear about the man who watched his wife being taken off in an ambulance to a psychiatric hospital? "I just don't understand it," he said. "All she did was stay in the kitchen and work with the children."

We watch folks leaving the church and say something similar. "I just don't understand it. They were working so hard and growing so much!" I'll tell you what happened: We have taken the joy and freedom of the new Christian and put a saddle of legalism, laws, and religion on them, and have ridden that horse until it almost dies.

IS HE REALLY SO DISAPPOINTED?

Christian teachers always seem to be pointing out Jesus' disappointment with our lack of commitment, our shallow theology, and our selling out to the culture. I suppose some of those charges are true.

The interesting thing about the anger of Jesus, however, is that he hardly ever directed it at the "bad" people, those who weren't committed and religious and who didn't have a correct godly worldview. Matthew and Luke called him a friend of "tax collectors and sinners." In fact, they tell us that Jesus hung out with the worst people so often that some observers started calling him a glutton and winebibber.[2] Jesus reserved his harshest criticism for the religious folks who "tie up heavy burdens, hard to bear, and lay them on people's shoulders."[3]

Let me give you the good news. Once while Jesus visited his hometown, the folks in his church asked him to read the Bible. He read a particular passage and then said—with a high degree of arrogance unless, of course, he really was who he said he was—that he fulfilled the Scripture he had just read. You could think of it as his personal job description:

> The Spirit of the Lord is upon me,
>   because he has anointed me
>   to proclaim good news to the poor.
> He has sent me to proclaim liberty to
>   the captives
>   and recovering of sight to the blind,
> to set at liberty those who are oppressed,
>   to proclaim the year of the Lord's favor.[4]

Now, that's good news! In fact, the incarnation of God in Christ was the best news the world has ever heard. It cut through the sham and pretense of spurious religious ideas. It presented the simple message that God was *not* what every religious person thought he was. And it offered people freedom . . . and with freedom, healing, meaning, immortality, and forgiveness.

WHAT HAS HAPPENED?

What in the world has happened? How have we taken a message that was so good, so exciting, and so freeing and made it into a religion that creates people who seem to have been given a misery pill and instructed to medicate the rest of the world?

How did we get so religious? Where did we go wrong? Where did all the layers of rules and regulations come from? How is it that being forgiven has made us feel so guilty, being loved has made us so uptight, and being free has made us so bound? How did sinners who have been forgiven repeatedly become judges?

I want to tell you a story. Actually, it isn't my story. I wish it were. It is Calvin Miller's story from his wonderful book *An Owner's Manual for an Unfinished Soul,* and it is about apple stealing. Because what I want to say in the rest of this chapter is so difficult to say, so hard to understand, and so hard to pin down, I think Calvin's story may help a lot.

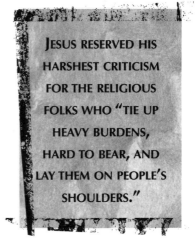

JESUS RESERVED HIS HARSHEST CRITICISM FOR THE RELIGIOUS FOLKS WHO "TIE UP HEAVY BURDENS, HARD TO BEAR, AND LAY THEM ON PEOPLE'S SHOULDERS."

When you read the story, don't get picky on me. If you're a Protestant, don't get hung up on the idea of confession. If you are a Catholic, don't see it as a criticism of priests and confession. And, whatever you do, don't "go religious" when you read the story. If you do that, you'll miss the good news—and that would be unfortunate.

Just read it with your heart.

> Every day on his way to hear morning confessions, a certain priest stopped and stole an apple from the orchard that he passed. On the orchard wall was a sign that clearly said, "Keep Out, No Pilfering!" Nonetheless, the priest would steal the fruit and eat it on the way to serve his people. He always finished the apple just as he entered the confessional, throwing the apple core on *his* side of the curtain.
>
> A young girl named Cora also stopped every morning on her way to confession to steal an apple. Entering the confessional, she would finish the apple and throw the core on *her* side of the curtain.
>
> "Bless me, Father, for I have sinned," she would say.
>
> "How long has it been, my child, since your last confession?"
>
> "Twenty-four hours."
>
> "And is your sin the same today as usual?"
>
> "It is, Father. I am still stealing apples on the way to confession."
>
> "*Te absolvo.* Go, and try to keep away from those apples!"
>
> "I'll try, Father, I'll try. But they are so good, and I am so weak."

Every day the ritual was repeated. Every twenty-four hours the priest stole another, and so did Cora.

Finally the priest grew exasperated with Cora. "Bless me, Father, for I have sinned". . . : a very ordinary confession on an ordinary morning.

"Today, Cora, I refuse to forgive you. You keep on stealing, and I'm tired of forgiving you, for we both know you will do it again. You'll never change, you wretched girl. Henceforth, I do not forgive you."

"Please, Father. I am so very sorry."

"No. Before the cider dries upon your chin, you will have stolen once again. I counted 365 decaying cores on your side of the confessional. You are too wicked and apple-ridden to ever receive my forgiveness!"

The girl wept her way from the confessional. For weeks her guilt grew. She finally quit coming to confession.

Autumn came. Winter approached.

The fields around the church turned brown. The swans left the pond. The early daylight was heavy with frost. The apples in the orchard were very few and mostly in the top of the trees. The wretched girl, still unable to leave her addiction, shinnied up the highest frost-tinged boughs. She was about to pick an apple when she noticed some movements in the branches across from her. Then she noticed a black cassock.

"Father, what are you doing here?" asked Cora.

"Praying," said the priest.

"In an apple tree?" asked the girl.

"Yes, my dear, to be closer to heaven."

"Oh, that I came here to pray . . . I came only to steal apples."

"Wretch!" screamed the priest.

At that very instant the limb on which he was supported broke, and the priest plummeted to the ground. Cora scrambled down and ran to see if the priest was dead.

"Girl, I am dying. You must give me last rites."

"No, Father. I am impure, filled with harried and vile and unforgiven apple thieveries. I am too wicked to grant you the absolution that you need. May God have mercy on you, Father."

The priest died and went to Hades and burned in flaming cider for a thousand years—but of course Cora never knew.

A new priest came in a few weeks, and Cora started back to church. Once again she went to confession.

"Bless me, Father, for I have sinned. . . . I stole an apple this morning on the way to church."

"You, too?" said the priest. "Tomorrow morning let's both steal three, and we shall make a pie together. Who knows but that our Father in heaven shall provide the cinnamon."

Even honest thievery had recompenses. At last the swans came back and the fields turned green.

After Cora and the priest had eaten many a pie, they found they actually were beginning to help each other for support and prayed for each other, and finally both were able to quit stealing apples—at least they did not steal them all that often. Still, some sins are hard to quit, and confirmed apple thieves must help each other pass the best orchards.[5]

The church is the concern of God. The Bible says, "Husbands, love your wives, as Christ loved the church and gave himself up for her, that he might sanctify her, having cleansed her by the washing of water with the word, so that he might present the church to himself in splendor, without spot or wrinkle or any such thing, that she might be holy and without blemish . . . , because we are members of his body. . . . This mystery is profound, and I am saying that it refers to Christ and the church."[6]

My friend Mike Glodo, the stated clerk of the Evangelical Presbyterian Church, said that he went to Jesus once to complain about the church. He said to Jesus: "They are a mess. They are uncommitted, mean, and lazy. They don't care what you say or even about you and your honor. They are a stiff-necked people, and they don't deserve your love."

"Mike," Jesus answered, "be careful . . . she's my wife!"

The gospel ("good news") is God's gift to us—and yet somehow, in our efforts to be more than we can be, even when our motives were right, we have lost our way. We have become obsessive, bound, angry, judgmental, and neurotic Christians.

I believe God intended something very different. He wants us to be free. In fact, he paid the ultimate price to make us free.

Let's talk about it.

A Dance or a March?

The good news is that Christ frees us from the need to obnoxiously focus on our goodness, our commitment, and our correctness. Religion has made us obsessive almost beyond endurance. Jesus invited us to a dance . . . and we've turned it into a march of soldiers, always checking to see if we're doing it right and are in step and in line with the other soldiers. We know a dance would be more fun, but we believe we must go through hell to get to heaven, so we keep marching.

I don't suggest that we should start marching to a different drummer. I suggest that we aren't supposed to be marching in the first place.

While writing this chapter, I appeared on a syndicated Christian talk show to discuss a book I had written on the doctrine of the Holy Spirit. During the call-in portion of the program, a woman asked, "Steve, do you pray to the Holy Spirit?"

I replied that I generally addressed God as Father.

"Well," she said, "I'm glad for that. I feel uncomfortable with those Christians who pray to the Holy Spirit, and I think it's a sin."

That's when I did it; I think I may have offended her. I told her that God really didn't care to which person of the Trinity we addressed our prayers.

"God the Father," I explained, "doesn't say to those Christians who pray to the Holy Spirit, 'Hey, you can't do that! I'm the important person in this threesome, and you had better do it right or you are going to get into a lot of trouble.'"

You see, the lady who called had an obsessive need to do it right, to be correct, and to march instead of dance.

If you read the last chapter, you read my brief on giving up. In that chapter, I tried to show you why not trying to get better is better. I suggested that the only ones who will ever get any better are those who know God won't be angry if they don't get better.

Let me elaborate on that in the context of our obsession with being committed, obedient, and righteous. It's driving us to prison and taking away our freedom.

Listen! It's better to give up trying to be better because, in the realization that getting better may not happen, the focus of your life changes. You get out of the trap of obsessing over something that is, at best, secondary. And you know what else?

CHRIST FREES US FROM THE NEED TO OBNOXIOUSLY FOCUS ON OUR GOODNESS.

You start dancing.

New or Nice?

I must say again that I love the church. With Augustine, she is my mother and has given me much good. In fact, I could never have written the critique that follows if I had not acquired the principles and the reality to make the critique from the very church to which it is directed. I am not an outsider.

Someone has described the church services of American Christianity as a nice man standing in front of nice people, telling them that God calls them to be nicer. But if the Christian faith is about being nicer, it becomes moralism; and in that case, Buddhism will probably be of more help than biblical Christianity.

When one measures the veracity of the Christian faith in the same way one measures the effectiveness of soap—whether it makes you clean—the kind of religion (or soap) you use doesn't matter, so long as you're cleaner than you were before.

I have a friend who is a "better person" today because he believes he saw the ghost of his dead father. So maybe, if the goal is to get better, we ought to hold séances instead of worship services.

The greatest danger to the Christian faith is not our shallow theology, not living up to what we say we believe, or a lack of conviction. Our real danger isn't racism, sexism, or a lack of compassion. The danger doesn't lie in our disobedience or in our uncaring attitudes about the poor, the oppressed, or the lost. The danger with the church is not our political involvement or lack thereof. Those things are important issues, but when we define our problems in those terms, we will never cure the real problem. All we'll do, in effect, is to take Tums for stomach cancer.

When we become moralists, we miss the good news that our righteousness isn't the point. There is nothing wrong with being righteous, of course, but when that defines "real Christianity," we make a great love story into a methodology of socialization. In other words, we buy into the view that religion's sole purpose is to make people good.

My father would not go to church because he thought that very thing. He thought there were bad people (the pagans and the unbelievers) and good people (the Christians in church). Because he didn't think of himself as good, he refused to become a part of the fellowship of Christians. He thought that his going to church would feel something like a wet, shaggy dog shaking himself at the Miss America Pageant.

I can think of another problem with the "Christianity = nice people" equation.

I'm sure you've heard the question. It gets asked all the time of preachers and seminary professors. In fact, a lot of pagans ask it of their Christian friends. It goes something like this: "I know atheists (or Buddhists or witches or whatever) who are very good, kind, and compassionate people. Are you telling me that they aren't saved?" They add, "I know Christians who are hypocrites. They are worse than my atheist (or Buddhist or witch or whatever) friend—and you want to tell me that they *are* going to heaven?"

If the essence of the Christian faith is morality, then they have a point.

Of course, I'm not saying that it doesn't matter what you believe or how you act. I am saying that if the purpose of Christianity is to produce "niceness," there may be some better ways to accomplish it outside of our faith.

WOULD YOU LIKE SOME FREE SINS?

In the fourth chapter of Romans, Paul says that Abraham had been given "imputed righteousness." In other words, Abraham believed God and, because of his simple belief (leaning on, trusting, delighting in) in God, God's righteousness and goodness got deposited in Abraham's account.

Then Paul makes an astounding statement, one to which I've referred before. He says,

> That is why his [Abraham's] faith was "counted [imputed in the KJV] to him as righteousness." But the words 'it was counted to him' were not written for his sake alone, but for ours also. It will be counted to us who believe in him who raised from the dead Jesus our Lord, who was delivered up for our trespasses and raised for our justification.[7]

In chapter 2, I mentioned that, for a couple of years, some friends and I aired a very controversial, syndicated talk show called, *Steve Brown, Etc.* Our mission statement called for us to kill off some sacred cows, so it was fun.

We had a major goal, to say to Christians (and to unbelievers), "Christians aren't perfect . . . just forgiven." We tried to present an example of flawed Christians who loved Christ and remained committed to him. We often said that we were not doing Christian radio, but "very good radio done by people who happen to be Christians."

By far, the most controversial thing about the program was my policy of giving away free sins.

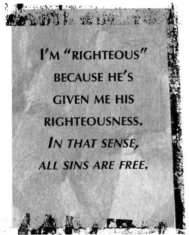

I'M "RIGHTEOUS" BECAUSE HE'S GIVEN ME HIS RIGHTEOUSNESS. IN THAT SENSE, ALL SINS ARE FREE.

When someone called for the first time, they got three free sins. If they called on a cell phone, they got six free sins. After a while, if I forgot to mention the deal, callers would remind me to give them their free sins.

On one occasion a woman called, irate about my policy of giving free sins. After she and a number of others had expressed their anger, Erik, the producer of the program, said, "Are you guys crazy? Steve can't give free sins. Only God does that. It's a joke. Lighten up!"

Well, it wasn't a joke; or at least, the joke had a very serious point: Our sin isn't the problem, so much as our stiffness. Of course, I can't really give away free sins—but God can. Jesus took care of sin on the cross (justification). And not only did he take it away, he gave us the great and wonderful gift of his (imputed) righteousness. That means that *all* of my sin is forgiven. I'm "righteous" because he's given me his righteousness. *In that sense, all sins are free.*

IS THIS CHEAP GRACE?

Often when I have written, taught, or preached something similar to "free sins," people call it "cheap grace." They will quote Dietrich Bonhoeffer's statement about God calling us to die. I like Bonhoeffer, but I also believe that he would be as upset as I am by the false charge of "cheap grace" when applied to the gospel.

I don't know why every time someone starts talking about the gospel, some detractor yells, "Cheap grace! Cheap grace!" Listen, if it weren't cheap, you and I couldn't afford it. If it cost us one thing— our commitment, our obedience, our religious actions, or anything else—it would remain in the store and on the shelf.

God granted us his grace because of the cross of Christ. It was a gift, given to us with a card attached, the message written in the blood of God's own Son. It is a gift that makes us righteous—and it has not come cheap. Nevertheless, it must be "cheap" to us—free, actually—or it would never be ours.

My friend Charlie Jones once gave me one of my favorite quotes. (Charlie and his wife, Ruth, are incredibly talented dramatists and sometimes help us with our Born Free seminar. They call their ministry Peculiar People.) Charlie does a wonderful dramatic presentation of Martin Luther. If you ever have the chance to hear Charlie perform that presentation, drop everything you're doing and go. It will be one of the most informative and delightful evenings you have ever spent.

Charlie reminded me once, when I was teaching on grace, of the time people asked Martin Luther about works of penance— works that naturally flow from genuine faith and trust in Christ. Luther replied that he supposed that was OK, but then questioned what kind of arrogance would make Christians think that anything they could do would ever be more sufficient than "the blood of God's own Son."

What kind, indeed?

How to Get a Life

If you really believed you were forgiven and accepted and that God loved you without any reservations, what would you do? How would you act? How would your religion change?

If I really could give free sins (which I can't) and I gave you three—no, a thousand—free sins, how would that affect your life?

Let me suggest the first thing that would happen: *You would be less obsessive about yourself and might even get a life.*

People who understand the good news about Christ don't always think about how they can be better and more pure. In fact, they seldom think about themselves at all.

I believe that, from an existential viewpoint, one of the greatest sin Christians can commit is a constant focus on their sin. It is a far more prideful and arrogant exercise than almost anything you can do.

When Martin Luther told Melanchthon, Luther's colleague and the composer of the Augsburg Confession, "Melanchthon, why don't you just go out and sin so you will have something to repent of," the great reformer was not encouraging sin; he was encouraging his friend to quit focusing on himself. Luther's oft-quoted comment that, if we sin, we ought to sin boldly, was his wise and wonderful effort to point out that our sin is not the issue.

I want you to do something for me.

For the next five minutes, don't think about purple flying elephants. Really—try to see if you can do it.

Caught you!

You're thinking about purple flying elephants, aren't you? The fact that I caught you thinking about them means that you will think about them some more. Pretty soon, if I don't do something to help, you are going to become obsessive and neurotic about purple flying elephants.

So, let me help. You don't have to think about purple flying elephants anymore. In fact, they don't even matter. You can think about them or not think about them as you wish. Thinking about purple flying elephants (or not thinking about them) won't help you at all, make you different, or affect your life in any way.

The late Gerald May in his book *Addiction and Grace* makes a profound comment:

> Through grace, with our assent, our desire begins to be transformed. Energies that once were dedicated simply to relieving ourselves from pain now become dedicated to a larger goodness, more aligned with the true treasure of our hearts. Where we were once interested only in conquering a specific addiction, we are now claiming a deeper longing, and we are concerned with becoming more free from attachments in general, for the sake of love. What had begun as an expedient attempt to reform our behavior has now become a process of transforming a life.[8]

Fixating on flying purple elephants won't help. But focusing on the God of grace and love most certainly will.

Let's Stop Fixing Each Other

What would happen if you had a thousand free sins? I believe a second thing would happen: *You would grow less concerned with the sins of others.*

We're going to say a lot more about this in a later chapter. For now, however, let me give you Jesus' words:

> Judge not, that you be not judged. For with the judgment you pronounce you will be judged, and with the measure you use it will be measured to you. Why do you see the speck that is in your brother's eye, but do not notice the log that is in your own eye? Or how can you say to your brother, "Let me take the speck out of your eye," when there is a log in your own eye?[9]

I'm a loner. If they would let me take my wife, I would become a Trappist monk (with a bit of theological hedging). Most of the time, I just want to stay in my study, reading and preparing.

In recent days God has allowed me to see that I want to be alone, because when I'm with other people, I try to fix them; or if they really get to know me, I will have them fix me.

A lot of Christian fellowship, Bible studies, and focus groups in the church are little more than efforts to fix one another. We become obsessive over fixing one another, almost to the point of mass hysteria.

No wonder pagans don't want to be around us.

A Change in Definitions

I think a third thing would happen if we all had a bunch of free sins: *We wouldn't have to define ourselves in terms of how good or bad we are.*

One of the most amazing, radical, and out-of-the-envelope things Jesus ever did is described in the seventh chapter of Luke. Jesus attended a party of religious folks, and a prostitute crashed the party. Jesus treated the woman with great respect and love. Jesus pointed out how this woman loved him—and then he said the following to the religious folks at the party: "Therefore I tell you, her sins, which are many, are forgiven—for she loved much. But he who is forgiven little, loves little."[10]

In other words, Jesus said that the godliest person at the party was a prostitute! How about that? I don't know about you, but that messes up some stuff I've always thought about sin and godliness.

I'm a Republican and did not feel happy to have President Clinton in the White House. (If you're a Democrat, we can disagree and still be friends.) I didn't approve of what he did in the White House with an intern. But do you know what I *really, really* dislike about William Jefferson Clinton?

I dislike the way he gave so many Christians an opportunity to be self-righteous: "I may be bad—a sinner and all—but I'm certainly not as bad as *that* man!"

May God have mercy on us!

The scandal gave us a wonderful opportunity to witness to the reality of the gospel, the really good news that God forgives sinners, "of whom I am the foremost."[11] What a tremendous opportunity we blew. We lost a wonderful opportunity to be free and to give others the freedom we have received.

But we were too busy obsessing over the sin of someone else.

In a wonderful and funny piece in *Christianity Today* titled, "Get Thou Over It!" Jody Vickery wrote about his pleasure in reading "letters to the editor" sections of Christian magazines to see who felt insulted. Let me reprise some of what he said:

> We believers are the most offended, wounded, upset, shocked, thunderstruck, consternated, and (the enduring favorite) outraged group of people on the planet. Is there something in the baptismal waters that makes Christians thin-skinned? Once I even read a letter from a correspondent that began "My wife . . . was disturbed." Well, pardon me. Didn't mean to disturb the Mrs. . . .
>
> Why don't we extend a little mercy to Christian authors? Jesus counted the raw immorality and theological imprecision of his day, not with sharp-tongued outrage, but with whispered grace.
>
> Sure, he kicked over a few temple tables now and then. But he didn't do it every Sabbath.

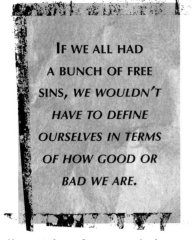

IF WE ALL HAD A BUNCH OF FREE SINS, WE WOULDN'T HAVE TO DEFINE OURSELVES IN TERMS OF HOW GOOD OR BAD WE ARE.

> And I can't imagine Jesus dashing off a quick and angry missive to the editor of *Judaism Today*. In fact, the only writing he ever did was in the sand. There may be a lesson there.[12]

One of the problems of cultural Christianity—wherein we lay down rules and regulations, measuring Christians (and ourselves) by how closely they (and we) come to conforming to those rules and regulations—is that it gets really hard to tell who is good and who isn't. I believe that our concepts of godliness have become so skewed that a truly godly person doesn't even know he or she is godly. For the same reason, I don't believe we know who is and who isn't godly.

It's a good thing too! If we knew, we would be so busy passing out meaningless awards that we wouldn't have time to dance. We would never get free.

A QUESTION FOR JESUS

If Jesus were to do another incarnation in our time, we would all have our questions. I don't know about you, but one of the questions near the top of my list would be, "Jesus, who is the most godly person living today?"

"I'm not going to tell you," I think he would say, "because you wouldn't even know the name."

Jesus once pointed to the scribes and Pharisees and said to his disciples: "For I tell you, unless your righteousness exceeds that of the scribes and Pharisees, you will never enter the kingdom of heaven."[13]

When I first read that, it bothered me a lot. You see, in my research I discovered that the scribes and the Pharisees were in fact, the most obedient and committed religious folks in first-century Jewish culture. In addition, the Pharisees were theologically correct in almost everything they believed and taught. Should we try to find an equivalent today, they would be the most orthodox and fundamental of all Christians.

I thought, *If those guys aren't righteous enough and if Jesus requires me to be even more righteous, I'm in serious trouble. I'm having trouble getting through one day without messing up so bad I can't fix it. How in the world can I be more righteous than they were? I've tried really hard, and I simply can't do it.* I was about ready to go through some very serious prayer and fasting . . . when I thought I heard God say, not unkindly and with a bit of laughter: *It's **my** righteousness, child. Not yours.*

Now go out and dance—and do it with gusto and with freedom.

But when he came to himself, he
said, . . . "I am no longer worthy to
be called your son. Treat me as one
of your hired servants."
—Luke 15:17, 19

CHAPTER
FIVE

THE MASKS WE WEAR . . .
and the Authenticity That Sets Us Free

DO YOU WISH TO BE GREAT? THEN BEGIN BY BEING.
—AUGUSTINE

I remember the first time I admitted that I was one of them. It was a hard thing to do. After all, much of my young life had been devoted to criticizing them—talking about their obscurantism and their lack of sophistication. They were the enemy, and they had done so much to hurt the church.

It was hard to tell people that I had joined them.

It happened on the long commute from Boston to Cape Cod. The five of us served churches as student pastors during extended weekends from Fridays through Mondays. And then, from Tuesday through Thursday, we attended the graduate school of theology at Boston University. Those were good days, and those guys were good friends in a way that only a regular round trip of 150 miles will make you. I was a theological liberal—just this side of whoopee—and theological liberals know things others don't know. It can make for a fairly tight fellowship.

I had struggled with the issue for months. And it would have been far easier and more acceptable to tell my friends that I was gay than what I did have to tell them. I wanted to be sure before I told them. There is nothing worse than identifying oneself with a disliked group, taking the heat of that identification, and then finding out one has made a mistake. So, I made sure I had joined the "enemy" through a thoughtful and absolutely volitional choice.

I had promised God for days that I was going to tell my friends; but somehow I never got around to it, found excuses not to do it, and generally avoided the subject. But I have this thing with guilt and responsibility. Given my nature, I just couldn't keep on pretending. It was interfering with my sleep at night and making me nervous during the day. Pretending will do that to you.

So, after weeks of shilly-shally, I decided to tell them.

"Guys," I said, "I have something to tell you."

Everybody in the carpool got silent.

"You know those fundamentalist types—the ones who are always beating others over the head with a Bible, telling people they have to be 'born again,' pretending they have all the answers? You know . . . the simplistic ones who think every issue can be decided with a Bible verse?"

Silence.

"Well, uh . . ." I said with great power and authority. "I . . . uh . . . uh. Well . . . I think I'm becoming one of them."

That was probably the most halting and unsure testimony for Christ in the history of Christendom. It was greeted with good-natured laughter. One of my friends said, "Oh, Steve, you're just looking for a soft place during exams. You'll get over it." Most of the others agreed. To my relief, someone changed the subject to the Red Sox and let me off the hook.

You're probably thinking that my admission was no big deal. It may not be a big deal to you, but I can still remember how relieved I felt to finally tell my friends my true identity. The honesty—as hesitant and as weak as it was—gave me a freedom that was truly wonderful. I had finally taken off the mask of my liberalism—a mask that enabled me to be accepted and feel acceptable—and I had told my friends who I was. What joy! What release! What freedom!

I remember thinking, *I will never wear a mask again.*

But I did. And the masks I have worn subsequently look quite surprising and far more disturbing.

MASKS OF COMMITMENT

The masks I've worn since revealing my true theological colors have more to do with my commitment than with my lack of it. Let me explain.

It starts with a desire to let people know about your faith, your commitment, and the focus of your life. But after you've told them, you have to maintain your witness. If that witness has anything to do with your goodness, your knowledge of spiritual things, or your willingness to be a model for other Christians, you are going to have some serious problems.

If you aren't ordained, don't serve as an officer in the church, or as a Christian leader in the community, you can survive if you really work at it. It will be hard, but you can do it. You may not be free and you'll possibly die young, but you can do it.

If you become a religious professional, however, it is a whole lot harder. Religious professionals have to wear an exceptional number of masks to keep their jobs. I have been a religious professional for most of my life, and I know all about masks. In fact, my intimate knowledge of masks and the damage they do gives me an insight you might find helpful. Someone who has been through major hurricanes can probably give some helpful advice to those who are going through small thunderstorms; or to mix the metaphor, a drunk can help a drunk. I've worn as many masks as anybody I know. I still do sometimes. That makes me an expert.

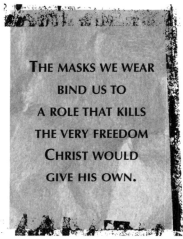

THE MASKS WE WEAR
BIND US TO
A ROLE THAT KILLS
THE VERY FREEDOM
CHRIST WOULD
GIVE HIS OWN.

In C. P. P. Taylor's play *Good: And a Nightingale Sang*, a professor of German classics, John Halder, is a kind man. He feels horrified that Goethe refused to send Beethoven money when the composer desperately needed it. He is good to his wife and to his blind mother. But gradually, Halder begins to sell his soul to Hitler and the Third Reich, eventually becoming the right hand of Adolph Eichmann at Auschwitz. He writes a novel suggesting that euthanasia is not all that bad and gets a personal note from Hitler, about which he feels very proud. Throughout the play a six-piece band plays music that matches the leading character's mood. It plays everything from marches to jazz.

Toward the end of the play, at the gates of Auschwitz, Halder realizes what he has done. He shrieks: "The band was real! The band was real!"[1]

Life is real. So when we go through life as actors and actresses, it may feel better and more comfortable for a while; but ultimately it isn't better, and the comfort is false. There is a great danger that life—real life—will pass us by and we'll die, never having lived. That would be sad in and of itself—but the masks we wear bind us to a role that kills the very freedom Christ would give his own.

Let's talk about the masks we wear—the masks that rob us of our freedom and joy.

THE MASKS WE SHOW OURSELVES

Believe it or not, most of us wear a mask we show to ourselves. Someone has said that the first person a con artist must con is himself.

Sadly, most of us view ourselves from the perspective held by others. From childhood we have learned to think of ourselves in a certain way that—correctly or incorrectly—constitutes our self-image. We put on that mask every time we look in a mirror. It shapes how we think of ourselves. We deal with life based on this faulty self-image.

But when you deal with life from the perspective of a false mask—one that others have given to you—you can lose the freedom Christ has granted. How? The false mask often makes your reactions inappropriate, your assessments flawed, and your decisions skewed.

If, for instance, I wear a mask given to me by people who called me worthless, I will react to you as a servant, thankful that you would even give me the time of day. I will become a doormat for every power-hungry manipulator I meet.

If, on the other hand, I think of myself as a spiritual giant, I am condescending to those who haven't yet achieved my level of "spirituality."

If I think of myself as a horrible sinner, a loathsome worm (wormology), I will start feeling guilty for the locusts that attack a crop in a Third World country.

If we don't know our true selves, we will live in a prison of false expectations. As a result, we will live up to others' expectations instead of living out who we really are.

The Mask of Unreality

Jesus is not into good or bad self-images, just reality—the reality behind the masks we show even to ourselves.

In the book of Revelation, Jesus said to the Laodiceans,

For you say, I am rich, I have prospered, and I need nothing, *not realizing* that you are wretched, pitiable, poor, blind, and naked. I counsel you to buy from me gold refined by fire, so that you may be rich, and white garments so that you may clothe yourself and the shame of your nakedness may not be seen, and salve to anoint your eyes, so that you may see.[2]

We hear a lot of drivel (and some wisdom) these days about the importance of a good self-image and the devastation caused by a bad one. I would suggest that the only valuable self-image is the one that reflects the reality of who we truly are. Anything other than that, good or bad, is a lie—and we will eventually have to face the truth.

In some school systems, teachers hand out grades, not for excellence or the lack thereof, but to make sure the child's self-image doesn't get damaged. Let me tell you what will really give someone a bad self-image. If you lie to a child about his or her ability, work, or demeanor, when that child hits the rocks of reality in the not-so-kind world, that child will feel devastated. You know exactly what I mean if you've ever watched an opening episode of *American Idol*, where talent-deprived "singers" express shock and disbelief when Simon tells them, "That was the musical equivalent of Montezuma's Revenge."

Did you hear about the mother who sent a note to her small boy's teacher? She wrote, "Billy has a tendency to be a bit loud and inattentive. He is quite fragile, and if you punish him, it could hurt his self-image. So, if he causes you problems, let me suggest that you hit the child next to him. It will get Billy's attention, and the example will make him better." If such advice were taken, we'd create two students with bad self-images. Why? Because in both cases, the created self-images would be lies.

The Mask of Superiority

Sometimes the mask we wear causes us to think of ourselves more highly than we ought to think.

I tell my seminary students that, because of their chosen profession, they are going to have a lot of opportunity to believe nonsense about themselves:

> People will tell you that your sermon was wonderful, when in fact, it died before it got to the first pew. They will tell you how spiritual you are, when in fact, you have the same spiritual troubles as the people in the pew. They will tell you that your commitment inspires them, when in fact, the day before you wanted to run away. If you believe them, you will become an empty shell. It will kill your ministry and rob you of the glorious liberty that is the heritage of a child of God. They will tell you, when you talk about sin, that you, of course, know sin only by hearsay. If you believe that, you will become a Pharisee and rob others of the liberty God would give to them.

The danger for all of us is that we will think we are better, more spiritual, and know more than others. Some Christians have such a high opinion of themselves that they think God is quite fortunate to have them. That would be of no import except that others, also because of a false self-image, believe them, making the church into an army of generals instead of a fellowship of people who love the King. Because grace runs downhill, it is very important that you not stake out your territory at the top of the hill.

Watch the people who pretend to be superior, and take care that it doesn't happen to you. When they pretend they are superior or think that others are, freedom suffers a major blow.

Of course, I don't want you to wring your hands and tell everybody how worthless you are. That can rob you of your freedom too. On the outside chance that you aren't as good or as spiritual as you think, however, let me continue.

I wrote a novel a number of years ago. I let some of my friends read it. They really liked it, because everything they think about me, they think through the heart of a friend. I also let my wife read it. She loves me. Everything she sees in me, she sees through the eyes of love. I had worked on the novel for almost a year, and I got a contract from a publisher. (I have no idea what they were thinking!) Once I got that contract, I told everyone I knew about my new novel. I also used illustrations from my new novel on the radio broadcast and in the places where I spoke. After all, I was one of a small number of great American novelists.

Then I waited for the publisher to launch the novel. Months went by. Each time I called, looking for a publication date, I heard that it would happen soon. Finally, out of frustration, I demanded my manuscript back, thinking that I would give it to a publisher that really wanted to publish "quality" material.

I got the manuscript back, as well as the cancelled contract, and then tried to place it with another company. I received a very rude awakening. One publisher said that it stank and that I needed to take some lessons from those who knew how to write fiction. In addition, my own beloved friend and longtime editor, Steve Griffith, took me out to lunch. Before we ordered, Steve took my manuscript out of his briefcase and tried to say something positive. The best he could manage was, "Steve, this may have some possibilities." Then, holding the manuscript up, he said, "There is stuff worse than this published."

You probably guessed that the novel never hit the bookstores. But the really bad thing is that even now, years later, wherever I go, people ask me about my novel and when it's coming out.

"Hey, Steve," they say, "whatever happened to that novel? I've been looking forward to reading it." Then I have to tell them, with great embarrassment, what I just told you. I hate it. If only someone had told me the truth in the beginning! If only I had known that I couldn't write fiction, I could have saved myself a vast amount of discomfort. It has been good for me, though, because God ripped off the false mask I was wearing.

But I still hate it.

If you have come to the place where you think you are wonderful and good and spiritual, when you really aren't wonderful and good and spiritual, you're probably in for it. As Revelation reminds us, there is nothing worse than being wretched, miserable, poor, blind, and naked—except, of course, not knowing that you are

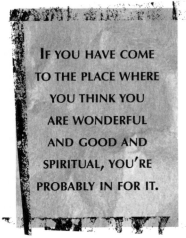

IF YOU HAVE COME TO THE PLACE WHERE YOU THINK YOU ARE WONDERFUL AND GOOD AND SPIRITUAL, YOU'RE PROBABLY IN FOR IT.

wretched, miserable, poor, blind, and naked. If you belong to God, he won't let you get away with it forever. He is the God of circumstances, and he will allow reality to break in on your fantasy.

Don't waste it. He's trying to set you free.

The Mask of Negativity

Then we wear the masks of false and negative self-images. These masks we fabricated from the material of abuse and shame.

Some of us wear masks given to us by a teacher or an authority figure who devalued us, causing us to spend our entire lives thinking of ourselves as nobodies. Some of us who have been hurt often and deeply wear masks defined by our wounds.

My father was an alcoholic, and my mother said that I was going to be just like him. My father was the kindest person I've ever known and my mother, the godliest. They were human, though, and something happened to me growing up that created a mask I still struggle to discard.

One time my drunken father threw a bowl of spaghetti at the wall. I was still in a high chair, but I remember what I thought even then: *What did I do wrong?* That was the beginning.

I won't bore you with the details, but all of my life, I've wondered what I did wrong. I wore—and still struggle with it on occasion—a mask of guilt. I accepted without question that most things were my fault; that I was mostly wrong; and that almost everything in my church, my community, and my world was my responsibility. The law of averages suggests that I was wrong, guilty, and responsible only half the time. Nevertheless, it was my mask, and I wore it like a martyr. Whenever I wear that mask, I'm horribly bound. My prison bars make me miserable and depressed.

What Should We Do?

What does one do about these masks—the masks of unreality and of superiority and of negativity—that take away our freedom?

Start by trying to deal with the truth of who you are. "For by the grace given to me," Paul wrote, "I say to everyone among you not to think of himself more highly than he ought to think, but to think with sober judgment, each according to the measure of faith that God has assigned."[3] In other words Paul is saying, "Don't wear masks that you show to yourself. At least be honest with yourself."

I believe the prayer God almost always answers for Christians is this: "Lord, show me myself."

Let me tell you how God answers that prayer: *He shows you how much you are loved.* He shows you his love—a love that is absolute, unconditional, and without any requirement that you do anything to justify that love.

After that—and only after that—does God show you the stuff you need to know about who you really are. You can handle any truth when you know you are loved and valued.

When I get critical letters from people I don't know, I ignore them. But when I get a critical letter from someone who loves me and has demonstrated that love, I am free to listen, to evaluate, and usually to change in some positive ways. The difference is in the person who shows me the truth. A true self-image includes some positive and negative aspects, but unless we get the initial positive input from someone we respect, we will never be able to deal with the negative.

A few years ago, I did a television show out of New York. The producer of that show was an atheist. I do radio because my face isn't designed for television. I have a perfect radio face. I do, however, have a decent voice. I often say on the radio program, "If I looked the way I sound, I would have a television ministry!"

At any rate, the producer said something to me that has meant a lot. "Steve," she said, "you're ugly, but your face has character." I've thought about that comment a lot. In fact, I've thought about it more than I should have. Her comment has given me a whole new view of myself and my looks. Before, I thought I was just ugly. Now, I'm ugly with character.

She doesn't know it, but her comment shattered a lifetime image I carried of myself, a mask of lies. I now know that I'm not half-bad in the looks area. While I'm not handsome, my face really has character.

If a mere mortal could do that much for me (and an atheist, to boot), think what a difference it would make if the God of the universe told me I was valuable . . . so valuable that he would give his Son so that I might be free. Every comment that devalued me, that made me feel like dirt, that made me want to run away and hide, would pale into insignificance in the light of the truth he spoke about me.

It is very important that you get your self-image from Jesus. He will never lie to you, and he will always love you. Don't ask

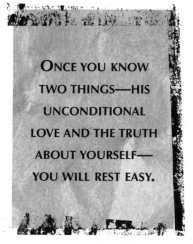

ONCE YOU KNOW TWO THINGS—HIS UNCONDITIONAL LOVE AND THE TRUTH ABOUT YOURSELF— YOU WILL REST EASY.

your enemy to tell you the truth about yourself. The enemy will use the opportunity to tell you that you're ugly and that your daddy cuts your hair weird. Don't even ask someone who loves you and sees you through the eyes of love.

Instead, go to Jesus and ask him. He loves you and will tell you the absolute truth. He will always temper that truth with his kindness and his grace, and nothing he shows you will change the way he feels about you. You will always be valuable to him . . . and ultimately, only he determines value. Once you know two things—his unconditional love and the truth about yourself—you will rest easy.

And you will be free.

THE MASK WE SHOW OTHER BELIEVERS

Wearing a mask when you look into a mirror will rob you of your freedom, but it is sometimes even more difficult and more imprisoning to wear a mask around other Christians. You may think that if they *really* knew you, they wouldn't let you be around them—so the best thing to do is to just keep on pretending.

That is a lie from the pit of hell. But before we consider how to counteract the lie with something more heavenly, let's take a look at the primary mask we show other believers.

The Mask of Acceptability

Harry Stein, in his wonderfully funny and delightful book *How I Accidentally Joined the Vast Right-Wing Conspiracy (and Found Inner Peace)*, tells about the first time he was called a fascist.

> It was Saturday, May 23, 1992, at about 9:30 EST. I know for sure because it was at a diner party the weekend after Dan Quayle's famous *Murphy Brown* speech.
>
> Now, times have changed a lot since way back then, with most everyone today claiming they more or less agreed with Quayle's basic premise all along; . . . even Candice Bergen, Murphy herself, now says so. And since it's precisely people like these who get to write history, they're on the verge of getting away with it. . . .
>
> So, when, inevitably, conversation around the dinner table turned to the subject, I took what seemed a safe middle course. Quayle may have had a point. . . .
>
> A journalist and writer, not particularly well known but one of those sober faces that turns up on network news shows from time to time, commenting on this or that, he could barely get the words out. . . . What did I want to do, stigmatize all those kids born—here he made quote signs with his fingers—"out of wedlock!?"
>
> "Of course not," I replied, as mildly as I could, "But would it really be such a terrible thing if their parents thought a little harder in advance about consequences? The bottom line is that kids need fathers."
>
> He was red now, literally sputtering, and it took him a moment to get out the *coup de grace*. ". . . when did you become a fascist?!" . . .
>
> For a few moments after the jerk's savage onslaught, I was reeling. But then I realized I was far from defenseless, having a lifetime's worth of my own moral superiority to fall back on—which is to say a nearly inexhaustible supply. . . .
>
> "That's how you argue?" I asked quietly, "By calling me names?"
>
> Already a couple of other heads were starting to bob slightly. I shook my own sorrowfully, and moved in for the kill. "Is that really how you respond to someone else's ideas?"[4]

Does that sound familiar? Change the names, the place, and soften some of the language, and you have a covered-dish church supper during which someone might hesitantly utter a thought or an idea that contradicts the "acceptable" Christian archetype.

You know it's true. If you don't believe me, if you are an evangelical or a Pentecostal Christian, then announce at a church supper that you are a political liberal or Democrat. Or, if you are in a mainline denomination, announce at an ecclesiastical meeting that you like Richard Nixon or that you listen to Rush Limbaugh. Or at a Christian testimony meeting, confess that you are gay and that you need help, or tell people that your sin is gossip and you don't know how to stop. If you are a preacher, say from the pulpit that you aren't sure about the acceptable interpretation of a particular passage of Scripture. If you are dispensational, announce that you aren't so sure about the Rapture or, if you are a Presbyterian, that you think Jews still have a place in the economy of God.

This is the point: When the requirement for acceptance in any particular group is to think certain thoughts, to act in certain ways, and to fit in certain molds—and we don't think or act that way or fit the mold—we tend to fake it. We put on a mask that says, "I'm just like you. Now, will you please love me and accept me?" I can think of hardly anything that will kill your joy and freedom more than wearing a mask geared to get others to accept you because you are acting like them.

Allow me to let you in on a secret: *Nobody* fits the mold, and most of us wear masks to cause others to think we do. The greatest tragedy of the church is that, in many cases, the most dishonest hour of the week is the hour we spend at church.

I'm not suggesting that we let it all hang out. I grow quite uncomfortable with public and detailed confessions of sin. Some things ought to be shared with only one or two close and mature Christian friends. But when we give the impression that we have it all together and live "one hundred miles from any known sin," when we preach and teach about sin with the implication that we are talking about others, when we seem to be anything other than what we are, sinners saved by grace—we do a great disservice to one another, and we become bound to the masks instead of free in Christ.

You need me and I need you. If we aren't honest with each other, those needs will go unmet.

Last week I watched an interview featuring several cast members of the once popular television series, *Love Boat*. One of the actors, Gavin MacLeod, played the captain on the series. His story fascinated me.

As a result of his work as an actor, he neglected his marriage, and it ended in divorce. MacLeod said that when he "came to himself," he called his wife, Patti, to see if they could have dinner. She invited him over.

MacLeod knocked on the door of his former home and at first got no response. He was about to turn away, thinking that Patti had rejected him—and given the way he had treated her, he knew he deserved it. But just as he was turning away, a smiling Patti opened the door and invited him in. "The dinner is cold," she said. "It's been waiting for three years."

Subsequent to that dinner, they were remarried, and as I understand it, he and Patti have a tremendous testimony of how God can restore broken marriages.

The interesting point for our purposes, however, is what MacLeod said about himself and his broken marriage. He had been an actor for most of his life, always playing roles written by others. MacLeod had researched and played so many roles that, somewhere along the line, he lost himself. Because of the roles—the masks he wore—he didn't know who he really was.

That can happen with Christians. In fact, I sometimes think that so many of us have been playing roles in the church we don't know our real selves or one another. Sometimes I think we have become actors and actresses having fellowship, worshiping and serving with other actors and actresses. Sometimes the production seems quite good, and at other times it is horrible. Nevertheless, it is a production. When the lights are dimmed, the stage is empty, and the audience has gone home, only one question remains: What was all that about?

The answer, I fear, is that it wasn't about anything important. It was only a play.

The Power to Stop Pretending

Christ can give you the freedom to stop pretending. Of course, superficial Christians—those who have been wearing their masks for so long that they seem sewed on—will probably reject you. Those who put you on a pedestal and worship there will feel so shocked they might, for a period, not want to have anything to do with you. Religious leaders into control will probably kick you out of their groups, because honesty and control hardly ever sleep well together. Those kinds of people will probably pray for you and give you a wide birth.

If that happens, celebrate. You have now determined who is and who isn't playing games with your mind and your heart. And you will feel surprised at how much easier it is to come clean about who you really are. It takes a lot of emotional gasoline to keep the mask straight . . . and now you won't have to do that anymore.

The apostle Paul showed me how this works. In most of 2 Corinthians 11 and 12, the apostle does some bragging. I know that many Christians want to put Paul on a pedestal, but try to remember that it was the words of Paul in the Bible that were without error, not who he was. My doctrine of Scripture suggests that the things he bragged about were true.

Verbal plenary inspiration (i.e., the Bible is all true) is important to me. But it is also important that I understand (because the Bible tells me so) that none of the people who wrote the Bible were exempt from the necessity of the cross. They were sinners just like me. (We're going to talk a lot more about that later.) So, if you read the texts carefully, you will discover that our heroes of the faith sometimes show their own sinfulness when they write, even though what they write is propositionally true.

CHRIST CAN GIVE YOU THE FREEDOM TO STOP PRETENDING.

And so we see Paul, the apostle, the writer of much of the New Testament and the first Christian missionary, engaging in plain old sinful and prideful bragging.

In those chapters Paul is not only bragging and proud—he knows it too. (It's first degree sin!) He writes, "I wish you would bear with me in a little foolishness. Do bear with me!"[5] (You can brag only in front of people who love you.) Then again: "I repeat, let no one think me foolish. But even if you do, accept me as a fool, so that I too may boast a little."[6] As if we didn't get it the first time, Paul says, "I say not with the Lord's authority but as a fool."[7] And then, one more time God allows us to see the pride of Paul and his own guilt: "I must go on boasting. Though there is nothing to be gained by it."[8]

Do you see it? Paul took off his mask. What was behind it may have been prideful and sinful, but he took it off anyway. God included this passage in the Scripture so we could see a model of someone secure enough and free enough in Christ to say what he thought, even if it wasn't pretty.

Freedom starts with one person deciding, even at the price of rejection, that he or she is going to leave the play and take off the mask. If you decide to be that person, you don't have to do it all at once. In fact, that's dangerous. You trade a bit of your soul for a bit of someone else's soul. You test the waters. A little honesty here and a little honesty there, and pretty soon the costume ball turns into a real dance of joy.

But *someone* has to start.

If you are a religious professional or a church leader, you are probably the one who ought to start it. I remember when I decided to try honesty from my pulpit. I suspected I wouldn't get fired because I had first tested the waters at my men's Bible study and with some close Christian friends. Still, I was nervous. I remember the Sunday when I said before a sermon: "Guys, if you've known me for very long, you know the text I'm about to teach you is not one I've lived out. In fact, if you want to know how not to do it, use me as an example." The congregation listened quietly. "However, this is God speaking, not me. I'm going to place myself under the authority of what God says, and I want you to do the same thing. Then, I want you to pray that I do better, and I'll pray the same thing for you."

Do you know what happened? The same thing that will happen if you get honest. People rose up and called me blessed. Well . . . maybe that is too strong. But when I left that church, they made a book of letters written by the people to whom I had ministered for almost twenty years.

I've never read all those letters.

I didn't read them because God had taught me I would believe them. In an attack of sanity, I realized that nobody ever writes bad stuff in those kinds of books. Do you think someone would write, "Dear Steve, I think you are a horrible preacher and a worse pastor. Your administrative skills make this church look like Jericho after the trumpets. I'm glad you are leaving, and good riddance"? Of course not.

But occasionally I do flip through that book and see one phrase over and over again (and, at least, in this there is heartfelt honesty): "Steve, thank you for giving me the permission to be free." Once someone points out that the emperor is naked, everybody knows it's true. And everybody will rejoice that they have finally seen the truth.

The church should be a place where we can say anything and know we won't be kicked out, where we can confess our sins knowing others will help us, where we can disagree and still be friends. It ought to be the one place in the world where we don't have to wear masks. And, should that happen, the world—where phoniness is the standard—will flock to our doors. Why?

Because freedom, genuine freedom, is an attractive commodity.

THE MASKS WE SHOW UNBELIEVERS

We have seen that you can't be free while wearing a mask—not when you look into the mirror and not when you're with your brothers and sisters in Christ. But it is also important to know you can't be free while wearing a mask in the presence of unbelievers.

The Mask of Purity

We hear a lot of talk in the church about the importance of our witness to the world. Our witness *is* important—but God does not call us to witness about our goodness or that we have it all together. We are to witness regarding the freedom and joy we have found in Christ.

When we tell unbelievers we are good or that we have it all together, those who know us will deem us hypocrites, and those who don't will think that Jesus accepts only people who are good and together. And then they will run in the opposite direction.

Few of us say it, but it's implied: "It is very important that we not air our dirty laundry in public. If we take off the masks, we will hurt our witness."

Talk about a lie! That is a very big one. Accepting the lie is one of the major reasons we feel so uptight and bound around pagans. We aren't free. Meanwhile, they want to be free, but one look in our direction and they know they are never going to get it from us.

> DO YOU THINK THAT WHEN YOU TELL UNBELIEVERS YOU ARE WONDERFUL, THEY REALLY BELIEVE YOU?

Do you know anyone who ever came to Christ through someone's purity? Do you think that when you tell unbelievers you are wonderful, they really believe you? Do you really think they don't know (at least those who know you well) you're a big-time hypocrite when you wear a mask? Do you really believe that, by pretending you have it all together, you are going to bring honor to Christ?

No?

Then tell them the truth. When it hurts, don't lie about it. When you aren't living up to what you know to be true, don't lie to yourself or to your brothers and sisters in Christ. But don't lie to pagans either. As someone said, "If you want to confuse people, tell them the truth."

The Ugly, Beautiful Truth

I have a Christian friend who fell morally. When she fell, she did it big time. She slept with her pagan boss, a married man. She wept when she confessed it to me.

I told her that God was in the business of forgiveness, but I also told her that she needed to do one more thing. She needed to confess her sin to her boss.

"What?" she asked. "I can't do that!"

"Why not?" I replied with uncharacteristic wisdom. "He already knows you are a sinner. Why not tell him about your Savior?"

She disliked my advice, but she decided to follow it anyway. She went to her boss and announced that she had a confession to make. He felt quite puzzled until she explained.

"Night before last," she said, "I betrayed my moral standards. That was horrible, but I did something even worse. I betrayed the one to whom I'm committed, who has always loved me—and I didn't even mention him to you."

Her boss started to get uncomfortable (he ought to have!). I suppose he saw an image of some big, football player type—maybe her fiancé—who wanted to kill him for what he had done. He got increasingly nervous as my friend continued.

"My betrayal was a betrayal of one who loves me without condition and, even when I've betrayed him, will forgive me and won't let me go. I'm not going to sleep with you again because of him. His name is Jesus, and I want you to listen while I tell you about him."

Do you know what happened? Her boss became a Christian!

This would happen a lot more if we would take off our masks with our nonbelieving friends.

The politicians lie to them.

The commercial advertisers lie to them.

Their friends lie to them.

The people they work with lie to them.

When Christians take off their masks, pagans get confused and generally ask questions. When they ask questions, make sure you have answers—and please don't give answers from behind another mask. It would be counterproductive to put the mask on, when not wearing it got you the right to be heard in the first place.

LET'S TAKE OFF THE MASKS

One of the professors at the seminary where I teach used to have a wonderful handlebar mustache—not one of those little weenie mustaches, but a really grand one. He shaved it off the other day.

I didn't recognize him. In fact, I didn't speak to him for days because I didn't know who he was. Eventually I asked one of the secretaries to identify the man I kept seeing around the seminary. She laughed and said, "Steve, don't you recognize him? That's Scott."

I've gotten used to the new Scott. In fact, I've grown to like him without the mustache. He doesn't care if I like him the new way or not. He is more interested in pleasing his wife and himself than he is in pleasing me.

There is freedom in that.

Shave off the mustache! Take off the mask. You have been bound, afraid, and depressed for so long you don't even remember what it was like to be free. I know, that's scary, and you don't have to do it all at once. But trust me on this: You will like the freedom it provides.

After all, you have to please only Jesus. And he is pleased with you. Not with your masks.

CURSED IS THE MAN WHO TRUSTS IN MAN
AND MAKES FLESH HIS STRENGTH,
WHOSE HEART TURNS AWAY FROM THE LORD.

—JEREMIAH 17:5

CHAPTER
SIX

THE PEOPLE WE DEIFY . . .
and the Truth That Sets Us Free

MAKE SURE IT IS GOD'S TRUMPET YOU ARE BLOWING. IF IT IS
ONLY YOURS, IT WON'T WAKE THE DEAD;
IT WILL SIMPLY DISTURB THE NEIGHBORS.
—MAJOR IAN THOMAS

I've spent most of my life trying to find people to put on a pedestal.

God has spent most of my life destroying the pedestals and reminding me that nobody belongs on one except him.

Don't get me wrong. There are a lot of people I admire. There are a great number of Christians I can look up to because they appear more committed than I am, know more than I do, and seem more faithful than I think I could ever be. But every time I try to make them more than sinners in desperate need of God's grace, God takes great delight in showing me the truth about my heroes. It is very dangerous to worship at any altar other than God's, and when we do, the inevitable result is a major loss of the freedom God would give his people.

THE DANGER OF HEROES

My friend and mentor, Fred Smith, says that one shouldn't pick a hero until he or she has died. That's wise. Once people have died, what they did or didn't do is settled. If you pick anybody alive, the story isn't over yet, and you might get an unpleasant surprise.

Publishers have often asked me to write a book on marriage and family. I always refuse for two reasons: First, thousands of books on marriage exist, and most Christians already know more than the authors of those books. Second, I'm not going to do a book on marriage and family, because all of that is still in process. While I love my wife and she loves me; while we have been married so long I don't remember what it was like to be single; and while I can't imagine any scenario in which we would ever get a divorce—one never knows what will happen tomorrow.

No, I'm not trying to prepare you for some bad news about my family. My wife and I have been together for so long neither of us would know what to do with someone else. I heard about an old guy who said, "I'm not looking for a young woman to replace my wife. I don't think I could stand waking up in bed next to someone who didn't know who Adlai Stevenson was." Besides the fact that my wife and I love each other, I suspect that neither of us wants to be with someone who doesn't share the same memories.

It could happen, however. Anna, my wife, could simply say (but probably won't), "Enough is enough. I'm out of here." I could (but probably won't) decide to get a Harley, a gold chain, and become a washed-out hippie. Our wonderful and committed Christian daughters could (but probably won't) become Buddhists, and our grandchildren could grow up to be serial killers (but probably won't).

When I'm on my deathbed, ask me about marriage and family. Then I might have something important to say. But even then, before you tell anybody, wait until I've been dead for at least twenty-five years before you chisel in concrete anything I say on the subject.

It is dangerous to have a hero who still lives.

But it's dangerous to have a dead hero too. I've given up reading "puff" biographies of famous Christians. When I've taken the time to do the research, I've discovered that those kinds of biographies have done Christians a great disservice. They create nonexistent people whose examples don't inspire excellence, only despair. If you are reading a biography of a "great" Christian, and that biography doesn't tell you the bad as well as the good, burn the book. It's a lie, and it will only make you feel guilty.

I remember when I found out that Donald Grey Barnhouse felt jealous of Billy Graham, that C. S. Lewis had a weird relationship with a substitute mother, that Charles Spurgeon went through months of depression and refused to preach because of it, that Martin Luther wrote anti-Semitic pamphlets, that . . . well, you get the idea. Each time one of my heroes fell off the pedestal, I was devastated—until I realized that God wanted to teach me something important. He uses sinful and flawed human beings because those are the only kinds of human beings he has available to use.

In my discovery I found an incredible freedom, a freedom that my putting people up on pedestals never gave me.

Whatever you think about the Bible, it doesn't contain "puff" biographies. In fact, God has been very careful to allow us to see the greatness *and* the smallness of biblical characters. Throughout the Bible, we encounter heroes of the faith with major flaws, serious sin, and embarrassing failures. Adam and Eve messed things up for themselves and for the rest of us. Noah got drunk. Abraham offered his wife in return for his own safety (twice). Sarah offered her female servant to Abraham so Abraham could have a son. Jacob was a con artist. Moses was a murderer. David was an adulterer. Jeremiah was a big-time failure. Rahab—an ancestor of Jesus—was a prostitute. Paul was contentious. Peter was a hypocrite.

A group of conservative political and religious leaders once gathered during the presidency of William Clinton. A mother asked, "What am I going to tell my children when they see our president acting this way?"

"Madam," said a wise rabbi in attendance, "just tell them the same thing you say when you read the Bible to them."

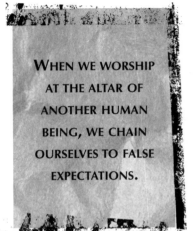

WHEN WE WORSHIP AT THE ALTAR OF ANOTHER HUMAN BEING, WE CHAIN OURSELVES TO FALSE EXPECTATIONS.

Can we talk? Our spiritual family is not the kind of family about whom one brags at a meeting of the Daughters of the American Revolution. God gives us the truth about some very unpleasant and sinful people.

Don't misunderstand what I'm saying. I am not suggesting that we should rejoice in the sin, that we praise it, or that we emulate it. God forbid! We do a great disservice to ourselves and to other Christians, however, when we pretend that anyone in our family has no need of redemption. The size of a problem can be measured by the degree to which one must go to remedy it. In the case of our sin, God resolved the problem by sending his Son to die on a cross as our redeemer. If we could be as good and as faithful as some would suggest, God would have sent a book instead of his Son.

AN IMPORTANT LESSON

Every time God destroyed the pedestals I had placed other people on, I hated it. But, unbeknownst to me, God was teaching me something very important, the same thing I want to teach you: *There are no super-Christians, and if you have found one, you have diminished yourself.*

It gets worse. *When you have demeaned yourself that way, you will find yourself in a prison of shame, guilt, and impossible expectations.* The false idol of super-Christians has destroyed the freedom of those who aren't!

Have you ever had a father figure fail you? Have you ever been disappointed after uncovering dirt on a hero? Have you ever looked up to someone, only to find out that he or she didn't deserve it—and then found yourself crushed? Have you ever discovered that a giant was really a pigmy, a Christian leader a moral failure, or a trusted and admired friend an enemy?

If you have ever had such an experience, I suspect you felt anger. "How could they do that?" you probably asked. Maybe you even confronted them with your anger and your disappointment. Perhaps you told others about your betrayal.

It may surprise you, but I think you were right to be angry, to confront, and to tell others. The problem is that you terribly misdirected your anger, confrontation, and witness. "Con me once, shame on thee," the old saying goes, "but con me twice, shame on me." The saying contains only a half-truth for a Christian. In fact, con me once, shame on me.

Why? Because Christians ought to know better than to worship at any altar other than God's. When we worship at the altar of another human being, we chain ourselves to false expectations about our idol and about ourselves. Our freedom to risk, to be who God created us to be and to think, feel, and act in freedom, dissipates in the face of the idol. Wars have been fought, churches have been divided and irreparably damaged, ministries have been destroyed, and God's people have been manipulated, bound, and hurt, all because we worshiped at the wrong altar.

Before I show you some of the ways our deifying people has caused serious problems, let me add this truth: Most Christians are not as bad as they could be. I'm a Calvinist, and Calvinists don't have a very high view of human nature. The Bible says that "the heart is deceitful above all things, and desperately sick; who can understand it?"[1] Most of the world's really destructive political, educational, and social movements took as their starting point the false view that human beings and human situations are perfectible.

They aren't.

While the Bible tells the story of flawed human beings, it also tells the story of how God used those flawed human beings in exceptional ways. The bad news is that sinful human beings are . . . well, sinful and human. The good news is that human beings sometimes do things beyond what one might expect. Paul said,

> But we have this treasure in jars of clay, to show that the surpassing power belongs to God and not to us. We are afflicted in every way, but not crushed; perplexed, but not driven to despair; persecuted, but not forsaken; struck down, but not destroyed; always carrying in the body the death of Jesus, so that the life of Jesus may also be manifested in our bodies.[2]

When we deify others, at least four specific plagues rob us of our freedoms.

1. THE PLAGUE OF IRRESPONSIBILITY

When we deify human beings, we allow ourselves to become irresponsible . . . and that robs us of our freedom.

Nobody is so wise, so pure, and such an absolute authority that you can turn your life over to him or her and thus avoid any responsibility for your own decisions and actions. But people do it all the time.

In the Family

I believe the Bible teaches that a husband/father is to lead his family. That is not to say that the Bible instructs the husband to act as the high potentate and sovereign czar of his family.

Some teach that a husband's abuse (no matter how vicious) should be accepted, that a husband's demands (no matter how ungodly) should be met, and that a husband's command (no matter how stupid) should be obeyed. Dear friend, that isn't godliness; it's irresponsibility. God didn't create wives to be doormats for their husbands, and God didn't create husbands to be worshiped.

A well-meaning Christian told a friend of mine that, in order to see her husband come to Christ, she should allow him to continue his physical abuse. In fact, she should accept it without complaint or protest as a call from God. That made me so angry I could have spit. If I had not been there to tell her that nobody deserved that kind of obedience, she might be dead now. I wonder how often women go through something similar with nobody to tell them the truth?

My friend had wrongly placed her Christian counselor on a pedestal. She had placed her husband on another pedestal. And in both cases, she was irresponsible—almost terminally so.

It happens with men too. I heard one wife make the following announcement when she and her husband arrived at a party: "George didn't want to come, but I told him that we were coming anyway." Then she turned to George and said, "Mix, George." George mixed. In fact, as he mixed, George seemed to have a good time in direct proportion to how far away he got from his wife. Even from across the room, however, she overheard him telling a joke and went out of her way to say, "George, you aren't telling it right. Let me tell it." He shut up and let her tell the joke. Then, as the evening progressed, she turned to George and said, "George, it's time to leave. Come on." George left. As they walked away from the house, I could hear her yelling at George because he had parked too far down the street.

I wanted to say, "George, don't let her do that to you. She's just as flawed as you are, and her views and desires deserve no more respect than yours." But he probably would not have listened. He had gone too far and invested too much power in someone else. After a while it's very difficult to change. It starts as an effort to keep the peace, and it ends in irresponsible submission to a deified spouse.

In the Church

The problem of irresponsibility doesn't happen exclusively in relationships within the family. Many Christians have turned over control of what they believe and how they live to authority figures. This is the stuff of which cults are made.

When Luke commends the Christians at Berea, he doesn't commend them because of their submission to Paul—who had preached the gospel to them—or because of their obedience to some authority structure. Rather, he says that they "received the word with all eagerness, examining the Scriptures daily to see if these things were so."[3]

I never understood cults—that is, until I joined one. While it wasn't a formal cult, it was just as destructive and just as frightening. Without going into details, it happened because I went looking for a father. And a man with a lot of money and a lot of power was searching for someone looking for a father. Over a period of almost three years, I managed to overlook this man's faults, to ignore his false teaching, and to defend him to everyone who could see what was really happening.

Sometimes I would compose a list of questions and concerns I had about our relationship, the organization he was founding, and the future relationship I would have with that organization. But do you know what happened? Every time I found myself in his presence, I would forget about the list and think, *How could I have thought such things about this godly man?*

I have a friend, Eddie Waxer, with whom I have had an

accountable relationship for more years than either of us will admit. (Eddie, by the way, has a wonderful ministry in the world of sports and recreation. Because of his ministry, the world will be different.) During my "cult period," Eddie flew in from Africa and asked that I pick him up at the Miami airport. We went out to dinner, where I described to him my involvement with the man, the questions I had, and the way I had handed important decisions in my life over to him.

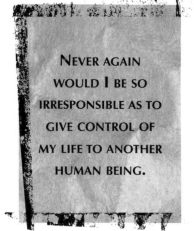

NEVER AGAIN WOULD I BE SO IRRESPONSIBLE AS TO GIVE CONTROL OF MY LIFE TO ANOTHER HUMAN BEING.

"Steve," Eddie said. "If someone told you what you just told me, what would you say to them?"

"I would," I said without hesitation, "tell them to get the heck out as fast as possible and never look back."

"Well?"

That night I made a decision about that man, but I also made a decision about my life. Never again would I be so irresponsible as to, without thinking and without questioning, give control of my life to another human being. I would always remember that others don't deserve that kind of worship and unthinking obedience.

Despite what I've related about my short-lived foray into placing my life into the hands of another flawed human, I always have had an authority problem. I resent authority, rebel against it, and try to avoid it. (Sometimes I even find myself getting angry at stop signs!) God is working on the bad side of that authority problem, and I'm getting better. So don't get me wrong. I'm learning to respect authority, and I know that Christians *should* respect authority. I'm not saying that leaders shouldn't lead and followers shouldn't follow. But the kind of unthinking and unquestioning authority that some neurotics demand and other neurotics accept not only violates Scripture, it takes away both our freedom and our responsibility.

Whenever a Christian follows authority figures who don't allow questions about themselves or their direction or teaching, get out and don't look back. Whenever someone says he knows what's best for your life, better than you do; whenever someone says that she speaks for God; whenever someone pretends to be anything other than a flawed human being who makes mistakes and sometimes gets it wrong—that person is sitting on a pedestal of his or her own making, and if you don't destroy it, God will. So many freedom-destroying things we do are connected to an irresponsible decision to allow others to be to us what only God is supposed to be.

An actor who played a physician on television said that, quite often, people would approach him for medical advice. "Are you crazy?" he said to anyone who asked. "I'm not a doctor; I play the role of a doctor. If you listen to what I say about your problem, you could die, because I don't know what I'm doing, any more than you do." That actor merely read a script for a television show, a script written by someone else who had checked the facts, who really tried to get it right, and who wrote with the help of legitimate medical consultants. That actor also worked under a director who helped him play the role.

Christian leaders and teachers are like that. We have a script (the Bible) written by someone else (God) and, we hope, direction from someone who helps us say and do the right things (the Holy Spirit). But, dear friend, when we forget about the script and the director, we do great disservice to truth. And to our freedom.

Does It Allow Questions?

In the sixties the cry went out, "Challenge all authority. Never trust anyone over thirty!" Now that the people who voiced that cry are over thirty and often in positions of authority, one no longer hears much about challenging authority. That is a shame, because many who came out of the sixties are teaching some really bad things.

So let me give you a principle: *You can accept truth and trust authority only if the truth allows questions and the authority allows challenge.*

It always surprises me when people invest wisdom and authority in me that I don't have and don't want. As I've already indicated, I do a nationally syndicated religious broadcast called Key Life, have written a number of books, and teach at a seminary. That sort of thing can cause people who don't know me to think that I am more spiritual than I really am and know more than I really do.

Sometimes our ministry will sponsor meetings in various cities where people hear the broadcast, and after the meeting I'll stay around to talk with listeners. One time a lady approached me and said, "Mr. Brown, I don't have any questions. I just wanted to touch you."

My wife, Anna, who was standing next to me, thought (and I could tell she was thinking it by the way she rolled her eyes and raised her eyebrows), *What are you . . . some kind of fruitcake? This is my husband, who has been as wrong, as sinful, and as stupid as anybody else. If you confuse him with God, you are going to get into some serious trouble.*

But Christian Leaders Are Different!

One last thing before we get off this first point about our irresponsibility. When we deify Christian leaders, we're off the hook because everybody knows they are "different."

My friend Dave O'Dowd once counseled a lady who had done something morally wrong. "David," she said to him, "I don't expect you to understand. You're a pastor."

David couldn't let that one go by. "I'm not letting you get away with that!" he practically shouted. "I'm just like you, and when you say that I'm 'different,' you get to make excuses for yourself. I'm just not going to let you do that."

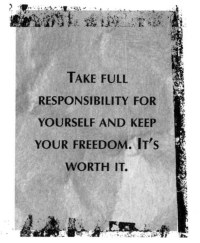

TAKE FULL RESPONSIBILITY FOR YOURSELF AND KEEP YOUR FREEDOM. IT'S WORTH IT.

We all try to do something similar at one time or another. If I can put C. S. Lewis (or anybody else) into a different category than myself, I can find some really good excuses for the way I am. Keeping a list of saints (without the truth of their "unsaintly" side) lets the rest of us off the hook. "Of course they were obedient. They were, after all, saints—and I'm not."

Don't let yourself get bound by such a foolish lie. Take full responsibility for yourself and keep your freedom. It's worth it.

2. THE PLAGUE OF DISSERVICE

Second, when we deify human beings, we do a great disservice to those we deify—and that robs us and them of freedom. We rob them of their humanness, forcing them to remain on the very pedestal that will eventually destroy them. When we deify leaders, we force them to live a lie, a lie that will make them both defensive and shallow.

The Loneliest People on Earth

Paul, writing about church members who tended to get puffed up with their own importance, said,

> For who sees anything different in you? What do you have that
> you did not receive? If then you received it, why do you boast as if
> you did not receive it? . . . For I think that God has exhibited us

apostles as last of all, like men sentenced to death, because we have become a spectacle to the world, to angels, and to men. We are fools for Christ's sake.[4]

The late Jack Miller, the founder of World Harvest Mission, tells about a time the elders in his church met to conduct some business. They heard a knock on the door, and a lady announced that she wanted to confess her sins. It seemed quite unusual, but the elders set aside their agenda and listened to her confession. When she had finished, one of the elders, with profound insight, said to her, "Now that you have confessed, what do you have to teach us?" Jack often said that only the repentant have anything to teach God's people. In fact, the most repentant person in a congregation should be its pastor.

Speaking of pastor types, if I mentioned his name, you would recognize it. This television evangelist has become the authority for countless Christians across the country. He often attacks others for their false theology; he gets very critical of those who disagree with him; he speaks with authority; and when he talks about sin, one gets the feeling that he knows about it only from watching others. This particular personality speaks quite articulately, and his views on politics, culture, and the Bible get quoted in many quarters as authoritative.

A friend of mine spent some time with this man. I asked him what this leader was like. "Steve," he said, "he is a good man, but he is the loneliest man I've ever known. He has come to believe what others say about him, and it's going to destroy him."

Isn't that sad?

We need to make a covenant together not to create that kind of loneliness and deception in the leaders we love. When they become puffed up with their own importance, their lack of freedom and their loneliness is as much our fault as it is theirs.

Free Them from Prison

My friend Harold Bussell wrote a very good book a number of years ago titled *Unholy Devotion*. At the time Harold served as the Dean of the Chapel at Gordon College, a prominent evangelical liberal-arts college. Harold said he had noticed how many students who came to Christian colleges tended to look to the chaplain to make decisions for them as a replacement for their absent pastor or other guru. He wrote:

> This kind of student usually comes from a congregation that has been built around a powerful pastor or leader. This phenomenon in the church is nothing new. Groups have often centered around a spiritual authority who has furthered his or her personal goals. Leaders of such groups often are impelled by genuine beliefs in their ideas, insights, discoveries, and spirituality as being the solutions and answers to the complex problems and ills of society. If the group believes that members can become sinless, the leader, of necessity, must be blind to the fault of his or her own impure motives in dominating and wielding power over others, otherwise their whole foundation falls. If the leader isn't sinless, what is the hope for the laity? This blindness and subtle manipulation and control is not limited to extreme cults. . . . Blind abuse of power is also evident in many Evangelical churches.[5]

When a Christian leader acts as if he or she has a hotline to God, speaks from Sinai, and knows all, don't listen to that leader. But even more important, do that leader a favor and tell him or her to repent . . . like yesterday. If nobody ever challenges that kind of unholy authority, it will continue.

When you affirm that kind of nonsense, you allow the leader to stay in a prison where it becomes impossible for him or her to be free. You will then be just as guilty for their lack of freedom as they are. It is a sin (to say nothing of what it does to the leader) for leaders to manipulate and take away freedom, but it is sometimes a greater sin to allow leaders to do it. You do yourself and leaders no service by allowing it. And if you love a leader, you won't.

Defuse the Pride

I teach a course in pastoral theology at Reformed Seminary in Orlando. (The course was formerly titled Practical Theology, but someone complained that was an oxymoron.) We devote one class section to developing a ministry philosophy.

From a lot of experience, I teach students that their ministry philosophy must take into account that they are no one's mother. It is quite easy, I tell them, to start thinking of themselves as a reasonable facsimile of God. "When that happens," I often say, "it will make you phony and empty. Those who follow you will get sick, and you will get sicker than they are."

I am not saying, of course, that pastors should not assume legitimate authority. There is nothing worse than a cowardly leader or pastor. But when leadership lacks humility and grace, it can lead to the pride that goes before a major fall.

My friend Rusty Anderson has a friend whose ministry was growing by leaps and bounds. And then, because of a drinking problem, he lost everything. He called Rusty and said, "I've lost my family, my church, my reputation, and my platform."

"Yes, you've lost a lot," Rusty replied. "But you may, for the first time in your life, have a real platform. Don't waste it."

3. THE PLAGUE OF GUILT

Third, when we deify human beings, it results in guilt—and that robs us of our freedom. When we invest in others an unrealistic goodness and purity, we open ourselves to a major problem with guilt.

Don't Use That Illustration

I have a great illustration on how servanthood creates authority. It concerns my wife, Anna. When our daughters were younger and working on their homework, countless times I'd hear them shout, "MOM, come and help me with my homework!" Had that request been addressed to me, I would have said, "Listen! If you want me to help you with your homework, come and kneel before your sovereign father and ask politely. Don't demand."

But do you know what Anna always did? Whenever they called, she came. She put down whatever she was doing to help our daughters with their homework.

One time someone had inadvertently left some grape juice in a glass. Anna poured some milk into it, and the milk turned purple. "Yuck!" one of our girls said. "Purple milk! I can't drink that!" I would have answered, "Kid, shut up and drink it. It's a new taste sensation." But Anna got up, poured the purple milk down the drain, washed the glass, and filled it with white milk.

Just when I would want to say to Anna, "Hey, I'm tired of your being a doormat to this family. Quit letting them treat you that way," I caught myself. I didn't dare say it, because I noticed the great authority she had. Whenever she wanted the girls to wash the dishes, they washed the dishes. When she asked me to do something, I did it. When she asked any of us to jump, we asked how high on the way up. The one person who has the most authority and the most power in our household is Anna, and she acquired that authority by being a servant.

Isn't that a great illustration of what Jesus taught in John 13 about being a servant? But I can't use it in my speaking. Do you know why?

Anna won't let me.

"Steve," she said, "every time you use that illustration, you make every mother in the audience feel guilty. I like for you to say nice things about me, but if you are going to say nice things, you had better also tell them the times when I don't act like a servant, the times when I yell at the kids, and the times when I want to run away. If you are going to tell them about the authority I have, you had better tell them about when I don't have any authority unless I use threats."

That was incredibly wise. A little later we're going to say more about guilt, but for now let me repeat that when you deify people in an unrealistic way, you set yourself up for guilt not rightfully yours. Guilt forges the chains that will bind you and keep you from freedom.

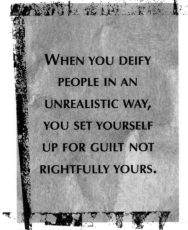

WHEN YOU DEIFY PEOPLE IN AN UNREALISTIC WAY, YOU SET YOURSELF UP FOR GUILT NOT RIGHTFULLY YOURS.

Don't Believe Everything You Hear

I remember the look on his face when he came into my study, right after an evening service. "Steve," he said, "I'm out of here."

"What do you mean?"

"I can't be a part of the church anymore, and I have to stop telling people that I'm a Christian."

I asked him what brought him to that conclusion, and he referred to a testimony that a man in our church had just given in the service. The man had told the congregation how God had delivered him from horrible sin and had bestowed on him the gift of holiness. He went on and on about how God had, by his grace, called him to holiness and had provided him with everything he needed for an obedient walk with Christ. I remembered his talk, because even as he gave it, I winced. Why? Because I knew the truth. The man may have gained victory in some areas in his life, but that was only a part of the story. He was a horrible and verbally abusive husband, his grown children wouldn't speak to him, and his fellow workers considered him an arrogant twit.

"Steve," the man standing before my desk said, "I just can't do it. I can't be that good. I'm having a whole lot of trouble in the area of obedience."

I couldn't tell this broken man the whole truth, but I did say, "Sam, don't assume that man is as pure as the impression he gave." Then I confessed my own sin to Sam, and when he left, he did so with the view that there might be hope for him after all.

What I did for Sam was simply to pass on the favor a dear friend had done for me. Remember, I've spent a lot of my life trying to put people on pedestals. I did that to my friend and felt comfortable with it. I thought I had finally found someone I could follow, a man who loved Christ with all of his heart and who obeyed in every area of his life. I asked my friend to be my spiritual mentor and pastor.

"Steve," he said, "I can't be your pastor. God is your pastor; I can only be your friend." And then, to my horror, he confessed a particularly grievous sin. He wanted me to know the truth. He feared that if I didn't know about his struggle, I would feel horribly guilty about my own.

The Lie That Keeps Us Distant

One reason I feel so strongly about this issue has to do with my father. My father was not a good man as goodness is traditionally defined. He was an alcoholic with all of the sin and degradation that alcoholism brings. Still, he taught me unconditional love by loving me unconditionally. That love covered a multitude of sins.

My father became a Christian three months before he died. His

Christian physician said to him, "Mr. Brown, you have three months to live. Let's have a prayer, and then I want to tell you about something far more important than your cancer." That physician told my father about God's grace, about the cross, and about how the Christian faith was for sinners, including him. I will be eternally grateful for that man and his witness to my father.

My father never went to church. Oh, he'd make a visit when my brother or I sang in the children's choir or did a recitation; but other than that, he stayed away. He never said bad things about church people. He never called them hypocrites or claimed they failed to live a life commensurate with their confession. In fact, my father thought just the opposite. He honestly felt that those folks in the church were good people.

My father didn't go to church precisely because *he didn't feel he was good enough.*

That makes me angry. It makes me angry with myself and any others who—maybe even without meaning to—sent out the message that there were good people and bad people, and the good ones were in church. By our self-righteous attitudes, I, and a lot of other well-meaning people, discouraged my father from knowing Christ, rejoicing in Christ's redemption, and being free to live, laugh, and dance. In doing so, we violated the very essence of the gospel.

I have devoted a significant portion of my ministry (and almost all of this book) to telling people that the only qualification for joining the "Christian club" is to be unqualified. And the only requirement for remaining a part of the club is to be unqualified.

4. THE PLAGUE OF ISOLATION

Fourth, when we deify human beings, it isolates them. It robs us— and them—of freedom. Autonomous leadership is bad leadership. When we put people on pedestals, the pedestal robs them of the wisdom of their community. The Bible says, "Iron sharpens iron, and one man sharpens another."[6]

We're All Human

In the book *Jesus in the Midst of Success*, Charles and Janet Morris describe a number of successful Christians who have learned to live by a radically different definition of success. One leader they describe is Doug Cobb, the founder of the *Cobb Report* and the president of a venture capital company. They write:

> Unfortunately, when "luck" seems to be smiling on us, unseen spiritual dangers often lurk beneath the surface. Cobb, a Christian, says the reason for that is no mystery: "Success blinds you to your true spiritual condition. People think you're wonderful. . . ."
>
> Even as a believer it's easy to drift into a self-confident independence. It becomes a habit to be always the benefactor, never the supplicant. As one pastor says, tongue in cheek, "It's hard not to feel superior when you really are superior."[7]

I have a friend who founded what became a very large church. He was—and is—a good and godly man. Because most of the people in the church grew up under his leadership and because he had been such a strong leader, the members of the church rarely, if ever, questioned his decisions. Eventually the church found itself in debt to the tune of millions of dollars, and by the time the other leaders realized how bad the situation had become, it was too late to fix it.

It is a sad story, and I'll spare you the details. There weren't any good or bad guys in leadership. As the dust settled, however, the extent of the devastation became clear: Hundreds of people had left the church, the pastor had been removed, the staff had resigned, and it took years for the church to achieve some degree of recovery. That church, meant to be an agency of freedom and joy, instead became a prison of obligation and fear. It didn't need to be that way.

My friend is a good and godly man, but he is also a very human man. Both he and his people forgot that. The pastor assumed authority, and the church people gave him the kind of authority no one can carry by him- or herself. Wise leaders lead, but they don't take themselves so seriously that they consider their decisions the moral equivalent of God's decisions.

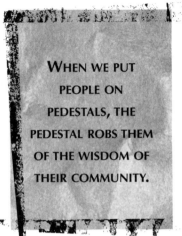

WHEN WE PUT PEOPLE ON PEDESTALS, THE PEDESTAL ROBS THEM OF THE WISDOM OF THEIR COMMUNITY.

The German philosopher Goethe said that men were most useless when they couldn't command or obey. There is some truth to that—but anyone who commands without accountability and anyone who obeys without question will go down roads destructive to both the leader and the followers.

We find great wisdom and freedom from the preacher in Ecclesiastes:

> Two are better than one, because they have a good reward for their toil. For if they fall, one will lift up his fellow. But woe to him who is alone when he falls and has not another to lift him up! Again, if two lie together, they keep warm, but how can one keep warm alone? And though a man might prevail against one who is alone, two will withstand him—a threefold cord is not quickly broken.[8]

I'm What's Wrong

One could cite any number of reasons why the English author and Christian apologist, G. K. Chesterton, was a great man. I suspect, however, that his true greatness lay in his humility.

"What's wrong with the world?" he once asked. "What's wrong with the world is me!" God has ordained only one Messiah per universe. You're not it. I'm not either.

Before we finish let me make some suggestions that will help you and others be free:

- When you disagree with something your pastor, bishop, or church leader said or did, respectfully tell him or her so.

- When listening to a Bible teacher, check the text before you accept the point.

- Ignore pomposity, arrogance, and pride when you see it in others.

- Ask God to fix it when you see it, or another points it out, in yourself.

- Be free enough to say no to authority figures at times.

- Ask to see the financial statements of the ministries and churches you support.

- Always check—don't ignore, as in *The Wizard of Oz*—the little man behind the curtain.

Those kinds of actions—and a variety of others you could add to the list—may make you feel guilty. Do them anyway. Eventually the guilt will go away as you start worshiping at the right altar. Then, perhaps, you will be able to hear God's voice again. In his words you will be free, and you will free others.

You should not feel guilty for doing something God does regularly.

You have heard that it was said, "You shall love your neighbor and hate your enemy." But I say to you, Love your enemies.

—Matthew 5:43–44

CHAPTER
SEVEN
THE ENEMIES WE DEMONIZE . . .
and the Humanity That Sets Us Free

IF I WERE A GRAVEDIGGER, OR EVEN A HANGMAN, THERE ARE SOME
PEOPLE I COULD WORK FOR WITH A GREAT DEAL OF PLEASURE.
—DOUGLAS JERROLD

First, let me say that I'm a conservative. In fact, I'm so conservative I think Rush Limbaugh is a communist. Not only am I a political conservative, I am a theological conservative—so orthodox I can repeat the Westminster Confession backward.

I have to start there, or you might misunderstand what I'm going to say in this chapter. I'm going to say we create enemies who really aren't enemies at all, and when we do so, we give our "creation" great power over us. That creation will take away our freedom.

I'm going to talk about tolerance and gentleness. I'm going to say that a lot of Christians become "serial killers" when they don't have to. You might even think I'm saying that convictions aren't important and doctrine doesn't matter. I might even be charged with selling out. Nothing could be further from the truth.

MY FRIEND, THE LIBERAL

A number of years ago, Tony Campolo and I did a weekly television show called *Hashing It Out*. The set was a diner in New York where Tony and I sat at a table debating political, social, and theological issues. I was the conservative, and Tony was the liberal. In fact, Tony and I don't agree on much of anything but Jesus.

Both Tony and I have busy schedules, and neither of us had the time to travel to New York to do the show. But we did it because both of us noticed a disturbing trend among Christians: how we demonize one another. We both wanted to demonstrate how Christians can disagree—even profoundly disagree—and still be friends, loving one another.

I think the demonstration was helpful. When the show aired, I heard one comment more than any other: "You guys really do like each other." We do. In fact, Tony and I have loved each other for twenty-five years . . . but we seldom agree.

We met for the first time at a Sandy Cove Bible Conference at which we both spoke. Tony and I had breakfast together, and I told him what I thought. "Tony," I said, "the only reason I took this speaking engagement was to be with you."

"Really?" Tony said.

"Yeah. You're an enigma to me because I can't understand how a reasonably intelligent Christian can say the outrageous things you say about politics and economics."

I knew if Tony laughed, we would become friends. He did, and we've been friends ever since.

Being friends with Tony Campolo, however, can cause you a whole lot of trouble if you happen to be, as I am, a political and social conservative. In the Clinton years, Tony became a close friend of and counselor to the president. In addition, it was reported (and, by the way, it wasn't true) that Tony was supportive of homosexual marriages. He also was called a heretic (which isn't true), a socialist (which isn't mostly true), and a wild-eyed liberal (which is absolutely true).

Let me tell you the problem. Just before the show started, I had breakfast with a colleague of mine who doesn't like Tony's views (a gross understatement). I said to him, "I want to tell you something I didn't want you to hear from somebody else. Next month I'm going to start doing a weekly television show with Tony Campolo and—" At that very moment, he started choking on his eggs, and after the breakfast fell so ill he couldn't attend any more of the conference sessions. My colleague told me his illness had nothing to do with my revelation. I, however, have my suspicions.

I like and respect my colleague very much. I feel sorry for him, though, because he is so bound. He has allowed his demonization of Tony to take away his freedom. One of the great freedoms we have—because we don't have to protect our goodness, our correctness, or our convictions (we just hold them)—is to love all kinds of people. When we can't do that, we hurt ourselves and become tightly bound.

I spend a significant portion of my time teaching the Bible at conferences and churches around the country. During the year when I was doing the show with Tony, I spent more of my time defending him than I did teaching the Bible. Almost everywhere I went (and it still happens even now), I found myself defending my friend Tony.

It always surprises people when I tell them about Tony's great concern for those who don't know Christ. Many of those who worked on the show in New York were not believers. A couple of them were atheists. (Remember the woman who told me that I had an ugly face, but one with character?) At least one cameraman was gay, and because of the way some Christians had treated him, he was not all that happy with Christians in general. In fact, some people on the set just couldn't buy into anything Christian whatsoever.

During the commercial breaks, I stayed at the table and drank coffee. Do you know what Tony did? He would take that time, often getting out the little New Testament he carries in his pocket, to talk to the people on the set about eternal issues and the importance of knowing Christ. I—the conservative whose theological and political views I genuinely believe were correct—sat and watched as my "weird, pinko, communist" friend told the lost about Jesus.

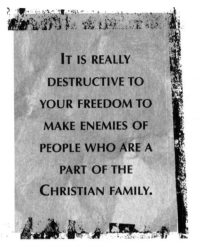

IT IS REALLY DESTRUCTIVE TO YOUR FREEDOM TO MAKE ENEMIES OF PEOPLE WHO ARE A PART OF THE CHRISTIAN FAMILY.

It is hard for me to hear people attack my friend. You see, I know Tony. I know his commitment to Christ, his love and concern for the poor and the oppressed, and his gigantic heart. I believe he is wrong about most things, but decided that I would rather spend time with Tony than with those who are right, who agree with me about political and social issues but who have become mean and rock hard in the certainty.

GETTING TO THE POINT

That brings me to the point of this chapter: *It is really destructive to your freedom to make enemies of people who are a part of the Christian family.* It is also quite destructive to your freedom to make enemies of most of the people outside of our family. In both cases they may be confused, wrong, sinful, needy, and scared—like us—but they aren't our enemies. We do have some enemies; but to make enemies of those who aren't is really counterproductive.

One more thing before we get into a few details of the way we demonize others and what it does to us. When I use the word *enemy*, it is easy for a lot of us to say that we don't have any enemies. When Will Rogers said that he never met a man he didn't like, he was probably lying. He probably could have said, however, that he never met a man who was his enemy. If he had said that, he would have been defining *enemy* in a very strict and narrow way, as "a person who hates another, and wishes or tries to injure him" (Webster).

When I use the word, I mean it in a far broader sense. I mean the neighbor who drives you up a wall; the atheist coworker enlisted on the wrong side of the "culture war"; the Calvinist (or Catholic, Dispensationalist, Charismatic, Arminian, Democrat, Republican, whatever) who you wish would just finally accept the truth or go away; or the man or woman at church who won't stop talking about you. When I use the word *enemy*, I mean a great variety of people with whom you disagree, for whom you give no quarter, and with whom you don't want to associate. For some of us it is gays; for others, the liberals; and for others it is anybody who looks different, who holds different ideas, or who expresses those ideas in the wrong place.

Let me give you a road map of where we're going to travel in this chapter. First, I want to state a principle to serve as the controlling, foundational guideline. Then I want to show you why demonizing others will rob you of your freedom. Finally, I want to share three startling statements that will help free you from the power you have given your enemies.

THE PRINCIPLE

Here's the principle that will serve as our foundation: *In general, we don't perceive people as enemies because of who they are, but because of who* we *are*. The biggest battle you will fight will be with yourself, not with the people you perceive as enemies. They really don't need fixing. And, even if they do, you're not their mother. We are the ones who need fixing.

HOW DEMONIZING OTHERS ROBS YOU OF YOUR FREEDOM

So what does the demonizing of enemies have to do with our freedom? Let me show you what demonizing others will do to you.

When You're a Controller, You Quickly Become "Controllee"

If you've read this far, you know that I am a bit out of the box. Because of the public nature of my ministry, I receive a lot of very critical and angry letters.

(On the broadcast I sometimes offer a tape of my testimony. When I mention it, I will often say in a kidding fashion, "I'm offering this tape for those of you who don't believe I'm saved." I once got a letter from a lady who I hope was kidding too. "I thought you were making a joke about people not thinking you were saved," she wrote. "But I told my Bible study that I listen to you, and now they don't think I'm saved.")

I have discovered that critical people tend to write very long letters. I used to spend a considerable portion of my time answering, point by point, all of those letters. But do you know what I found? When I answered their five-page letter with a five-page response, I received a ten-page response to my response. It drove me nuts until I finally realized that, in my effort to control what people thought about me and my views, I gave them power over me they had not earned.

These days I answer the really long and critical letters with, "Dear ____, You may be right, but you may be wrong too. Can we disagree and still be friends?" They don't generally like that kind of response. Tough! I'm just not going to play that game anymore. I'm free! And it's such a relief.

When I have enemies, I must control, change, or defeat them. That takes a lot of time; but even more important, I find that I have given my enemy the ability to control me and take away my freedom.

I don't have to agree with the homosexual lifestyle, with political or theological liberals, or with those who hate Christians. Still, I think I will, as Jesus said, "let the dead bury the dead" and just follow him. When I need to make a witness, I will, and when it needs to be really strong, I will make it strong. But I don't have to fix anything or anyone. That is God's business. When I let him be God, I'm incredibly free to be . . . well, his servant.

My friend Terry Mattingly writes a weekly column for Scripts Howard News Service. He tells about the time Elvis Presley gave a concert and, at its conclusion, a woman came forward with a crown resting on a plush pillow. She lifted the crown to Presley and shouted, "You're the king."

"No, honey," he said, "I'm not the king. Christ is the King. I'm just a singer."

When You Protect Yourself, You Can't Be Yourself

I spent the last chapter on this subject, so I won't spend much more time on it here. But it is worth a reminder.

If the gays are out to get me, if the liberals are trying to destroy my faith, if the apostate Christians are destroying the church, and if I am to do battle with them all—I can't be just the person God created me to be. No!

I have to become a soldier! I have to read the Bible to prove they are wrong! I have to prepare my arguments! I have to learn everything I can about the enemy! And I must never, *ever*, let my guard down!

And you know what happens? Pretty soon, I've created a prison in which I'm forced to live.

Not a lovely place. And not a whole lot of freedom there either.

When You Fight Battles, You Don't Have Time to Dance

As I write this, the nation is going through an outbreak of the West Nile virus. You generally get it from an infected mosquito. A number of people have died from the disease, and you can almost taste the growing fear.

Actually, not that many people have died from the disease. In fact, I suspect that more people die from falling telephone poles than from the West Nile virus.

But never mind! It is dangerous (the media tells us over and over again), and we must protect ourselves. Children have been prevented from playing in the parks in some cities. Teachers have kept their students away from the playgrounds. The stores have done a booming business in mosquito repellent. And a whole lot of people who used to play golf have taken up tiddlywinks.

I was doing a lot of that myself until I decided I couldn't kill every mosquito in Florida; that the odds of my getting the disease were about the same as my winning the lottery, even if I bought a ticket; and that mosquito repellent smells like a dog's bad breath.

So I've started living a normal life again. It's nice to be free of all that effort at keeping free of the West Nile virus!

We're that way about the enemies we create. There are so very many of them, and they are so very strong that I must not rest, let up, or back down.

I saw a bumper sticker the other day that read, "I'm woman, I'm strong, I'm in your face . . . I'm tired."

Well, I'm tired too. I quit. I now feel a lot better.

And I'm free.

When You Fight Demons, You Become One

Have you ever noticed how some folks with a ministry of exorcism of demons find so many of them?

I had a dear friend who died of cancer. As his pastor I had decided that God was probably not going to heal him and that I was called to prepare him for eternity. On most nights I would visit my friend, read the Scriptures to him, and pray with him. He did not feel happy about his death, but he was dealing with it.

One evening I came into his hospital room and quickly saw that all of the peace and courage that God had given him had vanished. My friend was angry and afraid. I asked him what had happened. He

WHEN YOU START LOOKING FOR DEMONS, YOU FIND THEM.

told me about a Christian man who had come to visit, who had told him that his cancer was the result of demons, and he had performed an exorcism. It took me days to point my friend once again to the God who loved him and who was far more powerful than any demon some misguided brother had dreamed up.

It's funny how, when you start looking for demons, you find them. There are demons of smoking, demons of cancer, demons of criticism, demons of drink. They're like weeds. They're everywhere, and you can't get rid of them.

(They remind me of the cords some of us employ to bind Satan. Odd thing about those cords—they seem to snap quite easily. The devil must go through a gross of them every day. But that's another topic for another day.)

It's also strange how, when you start looking for enemies, you find them. They're like weeds too.

The same tools the enemies use to fight you, you must use to fight them. And too often you become very much like the thing you are fighting. Christians are sometimes more angry, more demeaning, more critical, more condemning, and more manipulative than their enemies.

I have a dear friend who participated in a pro-life demonstration. Across the street the pro-abortion folks had their own demonstration. It soon became a shouting match with each side hurling vitriol at the other.

Then, to her surprise, my friend saw a lady on the other side with whom she had grown up. They had gone to grammar school together, and in high school they had been best friends. Over the years their lives had gone in different directions, and they hadn't seen much of each other. But there she was, my friend's friend, on the other side of the street, taking the opposite side of a very important issue.

My friend put down her sign and walked across the street to talk to her old friend. When she got there, however, she found she couldn't talk. She started weeping. My friend's friend put down her sign too. If you had been there, you would have seen two "enemies" hugging each other and crying together. My friend said to her friend, "Now, maybe we can talk."

Do you know what made the early Christians so dangerous? The world's power over them (ecclesiastical, political, cultural) had been taken away. They were free. That's why they turned this world upside down. They didn't have anything to protect and very little about which to fight. They made their witness clearly and often quite forcefully . . . and then they let the devil take the hindmost.

THREE STARTLING STATEMENTS

It's time for me to give you three startling (but quite helpful) statements that will help free you from the power you've given to others. If you aren't a believer, they won't apply to you.

Christians have some major benefits in the business of living and relating to others that unbelievers—by the very nature of their existential, philosophical, and theological worldviews—simply do not have. The tragedy is that Christians (and I include myself here) too often want to play the world's game, with the world's tools, and by the world's rules.

Jesus told someone who was making excuses for not following him, "Follow me, and leave the dead to bury their own dead."[1] When Jesus said that, he was saying that his followers didn't have to worry about a lot of the "stuff" pagans have to worry about. All of the things the world feels are desperately important aren't really so important after all.

But I digress. Let's get to the startling statements.

1. You Don't Have to Pretend to Be Good

Most people think, *If my Christian friends knew the way I really am, I wouldn't have a Christian friend left. My pastor would be shocked, my kids would disown me, and I would have to find a Buddhist fellowship in order to worship.*

Wouldn't happen. Do you know why?

Because they are just like you. People are my business, and I know.

Listen! You don't have to pretend to be a good person, because we both know that you're not. I know I'm better than I was, but God is still working on me; and the product won't be finished until we get home. When we confess to one another that we aren't good people, the necessity of my demonizing you—because I need to feel good about myself—is no longer a necessity. My desire to protect myself—by diverting attention away from myself and my own guilt and pointing at you—is no longer my desire. I don't—thank God Almighty!—have anything to protect anymore.

But when I protect something I don't have to protect, I find myself in a prison of my own making. And so will you.

I Am Jim Bakker

Have you ever noticed how Christians will talk so eagerly about another Christian who has fallen theologically, spiritually, or morally? Take, for instance, the fall of Jim Bakker.

I've interviewed Reverend Bakker on a couple of occasions. The most interesting thing about him is not him, but the Christian community's reaction to him. When nobody knew his sin, all kinds of Christian leaders made their way to Heritage USA to be on his television show. When we found out that Jim Bakker had been doing some really bad things, however, we were quick to point out to our nonbelieving friends that Bakker was not a Christian "like us." We wanted to put as much distance between Bakker and ourselves as we possibly could.

I have a preacher friend who, shortly after Bakker's fall and to the horror of those who heard it, preached a sermon he titled "I Am Jim Bakker." He made the point that "the saying is trustworthy and deserving of full acceptance, that Christ Jesus came into the world to save sinners, *of whom I am the foremost.*"[2] He insisted that no Christian could speak as an outsider of the human race. My preacher-friend's wife told me that she wished he hadn't preached the sermon because, she said, only half-seriously, "Now everybody thinks my husband's doing the same thing."

Let me tell you something interesting Jim Bakker said on my television program, *The Late Steve Brown Show*. We were discussing his time in prison and how diffi-cult it had been. Then I said that the hardest thing about the whole experience must have been the feeling of shame and embarrass-ment he felt. He smiled and allowed that it was very difficult. Then he said something profound: "Steve," he said, "I'm glad it all happened. Now I can go anywhere and be with anybody in the whole

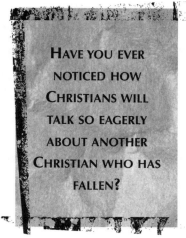

HAVE YOU EVER NOTICED HOW CHRISTIANS WILL TALK SO EAGERLY ABOUT ANOTHER CHRISTIAN WHO HAS FALLEN?

world, and there are no raised eyebrows. I can go into any bar—any social circle of outcasts—and nobody tells me that I ought to be care-ful because 'people will talk' and that I will 'hurt my reputation.' People have already talked, and I don't have any reputation to hurt. It doesn't matter anymore. I'm free!"

Isn't that great? Jim Bakker knew he didn't have to pretend to be good anymore. He knew he was a sinner. He didn't have to wear his silly mask anymore.

Someone has said that we ought to bless those who curse us because, first, they may be right, and second, think what they would say if they knew the truth. If more Christians recognized that truth, we would be dangerous . . . and incredibly free.

The Power of Honesty

I don't think students read Nathaniel Hawthorne anymore. He is a dead, white male and, in a time during which political correctness is more important than insight or knowledge, writers like Hawthorne are generally ignored. That is a shame because his novel, *The Scarlet Letter*, has made so many people see the power of honesty.

If you've read the novel, you will remember that Hester Prynne is required to wear the scarlet embroidered letter *A* because of her adultery. It is a long and tragic story about how a child, Pearl, is born from the sinful union and how Hester refuses to reveal the name of the father.

At the end of the novel, due to the untiring efforts of Roger Chillingworth—a real loser and the former husband of Hester—the truth comes out. The father turns out to be a young minister by the name of Roger Dimmesdale. The now-shamed minister joins Hester and Pearl on the pillory, revealing his guilt and the scarlet letter of remorse etched on his chest. In the final scene, Pearl (who had become a hellion) kisses her father and begins to weep, finally revealing her own humanity.

What a horrible price secret sin exacts!

But what if it didn't have to be secret? What if we recognized that the church wasn't a gathering place for saints but a recovery group for sinners? What if we didn't have to pretend to be good? What if we didn't have anything to protect anymore?

Do you get manipulated by people telling you that you aren't living up to your potential? I did, too, until I learned how to respond. Now I say (and teach others to say in our Born Free seminar), "You're right, and if it is OK with you, I think I won't live up to my potential for a little while longer."

What if we really felt that being human was OK? What if I could admit to you that I'm a sinner and that the statute of limitations hasn't run out because I committed my sin this morning? What if I no longer had to pretend to be good?

No Agenda but Jesus' Agenda

Chrysostom (A.D. 349–407), doctor and father of the early church, once wrote:

> Together with all other ills, I do not know how there was added to man's nature the disease of restless prying and of unseasonable curiosity. This Christ Himself chastised, saying, "Judge not, that you be not judged." Though we are ourselves full of ten thousand evils, and bearing the "beams" in our own eyes, we become exact inquisitors of the offences of our neighbor. . . . Judge nothing before the time. . . .
>
> What then? Is it not right that our teachers should do this? It is right in the case of open and confessed sins and with fitting opportunity, but even when with pain and inward vexation. . . . For these things He alone knows how to judge with accuracy, He who is to judge our secret doings, which of these is worthy of greater and which of less punishment and honor. . . . For I in my own errors, he says, I know nothing clearly, how can I be worthy to pass sentence on other men? And how shall I who do not know my own case with accuracy, be able to judge the state of others?[3]

When you don't have any agenda but that of Jesus, and you know that Jesus is Lord, you don't have to be uptight. When you are convinced that:

- we are a lot worse than we think we are, and God's grace is a lot bigger than we think it is

- we are really messed up folks whom a sovereign God has, for his own reasons, decided to love unconditionally

- grace always runs downhill

- power really is made perfect in weakness

. . . then you can hardly get upset when others, for whatever reason, point out those truths. You see, if someone calls you ugly, and you know that you really are ugly but no longer care, the statement ceases to bother you.

(Good thing for me.)

2. Christians Don't Have to Be Right

Quite a disagreement arose in the church at Rome about eating food offered to idols, about which days should be holy days, and about a number of other gray areas in the Christian life. Paul weighed in on the argument with these words: "Who are you to pass judgment on the servant of another? It is before his own master that he stands or falls. And he will be upheld, for the Lord is able to make him stand." Then Paul added some wise advice: "Each one should be fully convinced in his own mind."[4]

People who are "convinced in their own mind" don't create enemies of those who disagree. If you tell me I don't have and never have had a mother, for example, I'm not going to start yelling at you. I am certainly not going to challenge you to a debate, shun you for your wrong views, or call the elders of the church and institute discipline. I probably will call a good psychiatrist (or, for those Christians who believe that psychology is the devil's handmaid, a mature believer) to help you over your seriously psychotic state.

When I know I have a mother and you tell me that I don't, I see you as a candidate for the funny farm—and you will have my compassion, not my anger.

Nobody Left to Demonize

But there's another problem. If we persist in demonizing people, pretty soon, nobody is going to be left.

I have a friend who once took me to dinner. As we walked to the restaurant, he pointed to a mountain near the restaurant.

"See that mountain?" he asked.

"Yeah," I replied.

"Last year, after I had been a Christian for two years," he declared, "I climbed up on that mountain, looked out over the town, and said to the Lord, 'Lord, I'm the only one left.'"

"And what did the Lord say?"

My friend smiled and replied, "He laughed and told me, 'You've got to be kidding!'"

If you demonize those people who disagree with you, you will end up being the only one left. That will be sad because, first, you aren't right that often; and second,

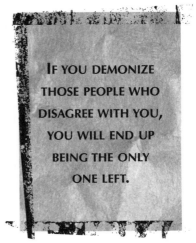

IF YOU DEMONIZE THOSE PEOPLE WHO DISAGREE WITH YOU, YOU WILL END UP BEING THE ONLY ONE LEFT.

there will be no one left to tell you when you are really wrong. You will encase yourself in concrete and call it freedom. It won't be freedom, but you won't know it.

Let me give you one more citation from the Harry Stein book I quoted in chapter 5. After he became a part of the "vast right-wing conspiracy and found inner peace," he found that some people—even family and friends—were not all that happy with him. Stein said that he had to be careful because gatherings of family members had "proven potentially dicey."

> I'm not happy about this. The fact is, we still fundamentally believe in most of the same things, and there's a lot more common ground than quicksand. Still, that tends to be forgotten in the frenzy of battle. More than once, things have broken down entirely, with almost everything anyone said getting sneered at, or viciously attacked, or, at best, misinterpreted by someone else. We're talking ugly.
>
> The same way this whole business known as the culture wars has turned ugly. It's like a barroom brawl in an old western that's

spilled from the saloon into the streets, the assorted individual fights—over gay rights, abortion, multiculturalism, affirmative action—coalescing into general mayhem, with even little old ladies looking for someone to bop over the head with a bottle.[5]

The danger with Christians is that, in our efforts to prove to others that we are right, we are liable to become "little old ladies looking for someone to bop over the head with a bottle." That is quite human. It *is* hard for those of us who are right to tolerate those who aren't. Only people who get it wrong sometimes, and know they get it wrong, find it easy to be tolerant.

So let's talk a little about getting it wrong.

On Getting It Wrong

I teach a doctor of ministry course at Reformed Seminary on communicating to postmoderns. When I started preparing for that course, I thought I would be making a brief for Christians in the arena with Philistines. I thought that a major part of the course would be teaching Christian communicators how to win arguments with postmoderns.

The more I read, however, the more I realized they had a point about a number of things. One of the things where they are at least half-right is the postmodern belief that words and propositions often get used as a way to get power over and to manipulate others. (Postmoderns are wrong about words having no intrinsic meaning in themselves; but that is for another book.) The more I thought about it, the more I realized that I have done that very thing on numerous occasions.

You see, I'm a teacher; that is my spiritual gift. It is a good gift, and I'm glad the Holy Spirit gave it to me. As with all spiritual gifts, however, there is a downside. The downside of the gift of teaching is that the person who has it wants to correct every error, straighten out every heretic, amend every sermon, and improve every statement. If teachers aren't careful, that desire can become obsessive. Pretty soon, the teacher won't have any students or any friends left. I've been there, and I'm not proud of the way I've disvalued people in my obsessive need to fix them.

When finite creatures deal with an infinite God and his thoughts, the very nature of the process requires that those finite creatures are going to be wrong . . . quite a lot. Paul writes, "For who has known the mind of the Lord, or who has been his counselor?"[6] If nobody knows the mind of the Lord, people who are terribly sure they do are simply wrong. God says, "For my thoughts are not your thoughts, neither are your ways my ways. . . . For as the heavens are higher than the earth, so are my ways higher than your ways and my thoughts than your thoughts."[7] If God says *that*, then it stands to reason that a fairly good chance exists that anybody who says they have it all right is, in fact, wrong. If you have never stood before God and been confused, then probably you have never stood before God.

No, I'm not saying that the eternal verities of the Christian faith are confusing or that the church has gotten them wrong. I'm simply saying those verities are far fewer in number than most Christians think. I'm also saying that a good way to make enemies is to pontificate from Sinai.

Have you ever been hugged by a doctrine? When you're cold, does a propositional statement keep you warm? Of course not. In fact, the doctrines about which we often fight are propositions intended to point to a person, and those propositions are valuable only insofar as they do so accurately. The danger is that we will confuse the propositions about Jesus with the person of Jesus.

I have the feeling that Jesus might save a lot of people who get the propositions wrong. In fact, I know some people who have all the propositions right who yet have no relationship with the Person to whom the propositions refer. The Bible says, "You believe that God is one; you do well. Even the demons believe—and shudder!"[8]

When we get to heaven, I believe God is going to welcome us with a fairly surprising statement. He is going to say, "You all got it wrong. And some of you got it terribly wrong. I've talked to my Son about you, however, and he says you're OK. So, welcome home!"

You don't have to be right. In fact, it would be quite refreshing for some of us to get it wrong more often . . . and to know it. Not only would it be refreshing, it would be quite freeing.

3. We Don't Have to Fight a Battle Already Won

Paul said that Jesus "disarmed the rulers and authorities and put them to open shame, by triumphing over them in him."[9] Jesus said, "In the world you will have tribulation. But take heart; I have overcome the world."[10] When the Bible refers to Jesus at "the right hand of God," it is talking about his authority.[11]

Christ is the victor. That means the battle is already over. And that means we might try relaxing just a tad.

Let's Not Get Our Knickers in a Knot

I recently received a note from a man who wanted me to write a response to a letter that had appeared in his local newspaper. He sent me a copy of the offending letter and said, "Steve, I don't have the experience to reply to this. Would you write something, send it to me, and I'll send it to the paper." The published letter came from a pagan not altogether happy with Christians. My friend said, "We just can't let this go."

I had just finished writing the letter for my friend when one of my staff members came in with an e-mail from a listener who wanted me to comment on a "Christian" poem. The poem talked about getting to heaven, where God will show "How I blocked Him here, and I checked Him there, and would not yield my will— There would be grief in my Savior's eyes." The listener wondered how I would respond to that kind of poem.

I said to the listener that we should not get our knickers in a knot. Then I had a moment of clarity and threw my own letter in the circular file. Both the believer who fumed at the Christian-bashing pagan and the Christian who wrote the poem of guilt-inducing drivel had misunderstood something a

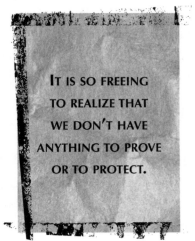

IT IS SO FREEING TO REALIZE THAT WE DON'T HAVE ANYTHING TO PROVE OR TO PROTECT.

Christian should never forget: The battle is already over. God won. It's final. There's no contest. Our side has already triumphed.

So why fight a battle with pagans who already have lost the war? Why try to make Christians feel guilty with something already settled? You can't "block" God or "check" him. At least, the Bible doesn't think so: "He does as he pleases with the powers of heaven and the peoples of the earth. No one can hold back his hand or say to him: 'What have you done?'"[12]

I share the concerns of the religious right, and I'm glad God has called some to stand for him in the arena of politics. I, however, am hardly ever involved with those kinds of things. Do you know why?

First, I don't want people who don't share my political and social views to think that I think I'm better than they are. When anybody believes I think that, I lose any credible witness I have to God's grace.

Second, I'm not that sure I'm right.

And, third, I'm a part of an army that doesn't have a war. What *would* happen if they had a war and nobody came?

It is so freeing to realize that we don't have anything to prove or to protect. We don't have to fix anything. God doesn't need any help. He did fine before we came along and will do fine long after we're gone. The great thing about being a Christian is that you can forgive, love, and encourage 'em all, and then let God sort it out.

A Method of Control?

I sometimes fear that many of us (and I include myself) find our definition in our obedience, in our ability to persuade others to be like us, and in our ability to win the battles. There is a lot of ego involved in being good, in being right, and as a part of the battle, having others know that we are good and right.

Religion can become, I think, a method to get power and control over others. That is what Jesus was talking about when he said of the scribes and Pharisees:

> They tie up heavy burdens, hard to bear, and lay them on people's shoulders, but they themselves are not willing to move them with their finger. They do all their deeds to be seen by others. For they make their phylacteries broad and their fringes long, and they love the place of honor at feasts and the best seats in the synagogues and greetings in the marketplaces and being called rabbi by others.[13]

I used to read that and think, *How could they?*

Now I read it and wince.

Even with the best of motives regarding the purity of the church, holiness, a concern for turning freedom into license, a fear that God's name will be dishonored, and a disquiet about the loss of values and truth—all of which are positive and good—it is easy to forget that the gospel is really good news. It is the good news that God has come, that he isn't angry with his people, and that he won't be angry with anyone who comes to him on the basis of the cross.

Whenever religion becomes leverage, it ceases to be the religion of Jesus. The gospel of God's grace takes away the leverage. Why? Because if I'm forgiven without condition, you can't make me feel guilty. If God loves me, you can't manipulate me by threatening to take away your love. If God knows my secrets and doesn't condemn me, then you can't use my secrets as blackmail. If you have power and threaten to use it against me and I don't care, then your power ceases to be real power.

Is there freedom in that? You tell me.

YOUR ENEMIES ARE MOSTLY JUST LIKE YOU

One of the good things about being a pastor (there are some bad things too) is the gift a great variety of people give by telling the pastor their secrets and their sins. They tell a pastor because they think he will be wise and helpful. Sometimes that's true.

But people also give another gift to their pastor when they share their secrets and their sins. It is the gift of knowing we are all pretty much alike: sinful, afraid, lonely, regretful, sometimes doubting, sometimes wrong, angry, loving, hateful, selfish, kind, wounded, and very human.

Remember my preacher friend who delivered the sermon "I Am Jim Bakker"? He taught me that nobody can speak as an outsider of the human race. When I learned that, I was so relieved. I was free of my enemies.

He Is Like Me

I remember the day the press reported that Bill Clinton's mother had died. Instead of my usual practice of thinking of him as a

Democrat, as a president who had championed policies I found abhorrent, as a man who had sinned horribly and who should be forced to pay the price for his public sin—I thought about the day my mother died and how I felt at the time.

My mother was an unusual lady. She was one of the finest and most earthy Christians I have ever known, a woman who affected my life deeply. She helped the homeless before it became an "in" cause. She reached out to people nobody else liked. She served her church faithfully. She loved the unlovely—and she could be very mean.

She read the Bible in the morning, Spurgeon in the evening, and taught me to cuss in between. I love her very much and still miss her terribly. (By the way, my mother was a Democrat, but now that she's in heaven she knows the truth. Hey, don't get so uptight. It's just a joke!)

At any rate, when my mother died, I sat beside her deathbed and wept. When I heard about the death of President Clinton's mother, I thought, *He is weeping the way I wept. He is bereft the way I was bereft. He is lonely the way I was lonely. He is going through the same thing I went through when my mother died. He is like me.*

I am still a Republican, but I'm no longer as bound as I was by Bill Clinton and those like him. I had given him the power to take away my freedom. But now that I know the truth about him, I'm free.

Someone You'd Like

I think Anne Lamott is someone you would like. She is a recipient of the Guggenheim Fellowship. She is also a single mother, a former drug and alcohol abuser, and one of the most gifted writers in America. She is also a Christian.

The story of how she became a follower of Jesus and her struggle to live out the reality of her relationship with Christ is chronicled in her wonderful book *Traveling Mercies.* It quickly reveals that Anne Lamott is a liberal and that her language hasn't yet been converted. But, what a writer! And what a lover of Christ! Anne Lamott is also one of the most honest and most vulnerable individuals I've ever met.

She's one of my closest friends. Well, that is a bit of exaggeration. I did, however, talk to her once on the phone.

I taped an interview with Anne Lamott for an afternoon talk show. I was to call her at the hotel where she spoke at a writers' conference. When I finally reached her, it became quite clear that a radio interview was the last thing in the world she wanted to do.

"I forgot about the interview," she said. "I'm sorry. I've just gotten in because I missed a flight. It was a long trip, and I'm very tired. Could we keep this short?"

> WHEN I HEARD ABOUT THE DEATH OF PRESIDENT CLINTON'S MOTHER, I THOUGHT, *HE IS WEEPING THE WAY I WEPT.*

"OK," I said. "But there is something I need to tell you before we do this interview. Do you know those fundamentalists who beat others over the head with a Bible?"

"Yes."

"Do you know the religious people who are to the right of Genghis Khan?"

"Yes."

"Well," I said, "I'm one of them. But before you hang up, I want you to know that I loved your book. I have never read a book that caused me to laugh and cry as much. I saw Jesus in your book in a new and wonderful way. I liked it so much I've given it to all my friends."

(If you buy an author's book and give it to your friends—trust me on this—that author will not hang up on you. So we started the interview.)

As I talked to Ms. Lamott, it became evident that, while we didn't have much in common politically or socially, we both loved Christ and we liked each other. In fact, what had begun with Ms. Lamott telling me to keep it short became one of the longest interviews I've ever done. I couldn't get her to stop talking, and I didn't want her to.

Finally, we had no more time, and I had to end the interview. Before we hung up, she said something to me I've treasured ever since. "Steve," she said, "this has been fun. Do you know what we would do if we ever met in person?"

I allowed that I didn't.

"We would," she said, laughing, "hold hands and tell each other stories about Jesus."

I wonder—how many "enemies" like that could you use?

NOW WHEN THEY SAW THE BOLDNESS
OF PETER AND JOHN, AND PERCEIVED
THAT THEY WERE UNEDUCATED,
COMMON MEN, THEY WERE ASTONISHED.
AND THEY RECOGNIZED THAT THEY
HAD BEEN WITH JESUS.
—ACTS 4:13

CHAPTER
EIGHT
THE BOLDNESS WE FEAR ...
and the Courage That Sets Us Free

IF YOU CHRISTIANS EVER GET OVER YOUR FEAR,
YOU'RE GOING TO BE DANGEROUS.
—AFRICAN AMERICAN BISHOP, WASHINGTON FOR JESUS RALLY

Christians can be dangerous!

No, not those.

The real ones.

The weenies aren't dangerous. They are irrelevant. But those Christians who have discovered they don't have anything to protect and nothing to lose, who have learned that Jesus is Lord and that it doesn't matter what others think about them or do to them—they are dangerous . . . *really* dangerous.

If you thought the last chapter was a call to niceness, you misunderstood what I was saying. Let me straighten it out.

Jesus didn't die to make Christians nice. Gentle? Yes. Kind? Yes. Loving? Free? Of course. But *not* nice! In fact, if you read the last chapter and have internalized what I shared there, you are now free to be bold. Sometimes boldness can be seen as quite offensive.

A PROBLEM THAT NEEDS ADDRESSING

The ministry with which I'm involved (Key Life Network) sponsors a Born Free seminar in various places around the country. Part of that seminar features a section on assertiveness training for Christians. The very fact that it is a part of the seminar creates controversy in some circles. Why, people ask, would Christians need assertiveness training? Aren't Christians supposed to be different from the world? How can assertiveness bring honor to Christ?

The very fact that those questions get asked suggests we have a problem in the church that needs addressing. Something has happened in the church, and it isn't good.

It is not that we don't have some leaders who are aggressive, manipulative, and power hungry. It is not that we don't have neurotics in the church who are critical, angry, and mean. The real problem is that we have people in the church who let these leaders and neurotics get away with being aggressive, manipulative, power hungry, critical, angry, and mean.

There is a problem in the world too. Some people believe that we agree with the "spiritual" nonsense that some call "Christian," with worldviews that destroy and imprison the poor and the wounded, with silly propositions passed as truth, and with shallow thinking that passes for philosophy. Our problem is that we have said nothing to disabuse people of such views.

My friend Norm Evans tells about the time a freshman lineman on the college football team came to the coach in the middle of a game and said, "Coach, they keep pulling my helmet down over my eyes. What should I do?"

"Son," the coach replied, "don't let them."

This chapter addresses the question "Why are we so bound and so imprisoned that we feel afraid to speak up, stand up, and be

Christ's witness in the church and in the world?"

In other words, if we're free, why don't we use our freedom to be bold?

A Few Questions

Since I'm posing questions, let me ask you a few. Be honest in your answers.

Question One: *When was the last time you said no to something someone asked you to do in or for the church without feeling the need to explain yourself?*

We ask people in our Born Free seminar to say no to a request, without saying anything more than a simple no (Matthew 5:37; James 5:12). One man told me that as soon as he said no, he found within himself an incredible and irresistible urge to offer an explanation to the leader—he had family obligations, he was already out four nights a week, he was already overcommitted, and his wife had threatened divorce. "Steve," he said, "I almost bit my tongue off to keep from explaining myself."

Try it. Just say no. And then wait. Since the Christian subculture expects you to explain yourself, the person who asks will wait for your explanation. But you don't need to give one. Just let your no be no.

Question Two: *Have you ever had an opinion different from your social group (Christian or pagan) and kept your views to yourself because you feared rejection?*

More foolish ideas and views than you can imagine have been allowed to perpetuate themselves on the people of God for the simple reason that those inane ideas and views have gone unchallenged. Some church programs continue for years, long after they should have been given a decent burial, for no other reason than no one wants to ask, "Why are we doing this? None of us wants to do it, and yet we keep doing it." When an outdated and no longer productive church program gets into trouble, we appoint a future-development committee to decide how we can salvage something that should not be salvaged.

I was the pastor of a church in which some of the brethren decided we needed a seniors' ministry. Two or three people sponsored a luncheon at the church for the seniors. It was a nice luncheon, and people seemed to enjoy themselves.

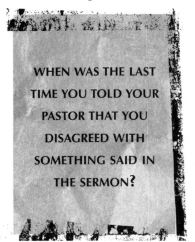

WHEN WAS THE LAST TIME YOU TOLD YOUR PASTOR THAT YOU DISAGREED WITH SOMETHING SAID IN THE SERMON?

After the luncheon one of the people with the vision said that it was time to elect officers. One older guy in the back said, "Officers? What are we going to elect officers for? I thought we were just having lunch."

"Well," said the leader, "if we're going to have an organization we need officers."

A woman in the front said, "I didn't know we were going to have an organization. I'm already a part of ten organizations, and I don't want to be a part of five of them. What in the world do I want to be in another organization for? What would we do if we formed an organization?"

The leader—the one with a vision for the new seniors' ministry—realized that he was quickly losing control and tried to inspire the people. "Look," he said, "we need fellowship, and there are lots of fun things we could do. We could organize shopping trips to Atlanta and in the fall go to the mountains to look at the trees."

"You've got to be kidding," said the man in the back. "I've already got more friends than I want. I can go shopping by myself. I'm not helpless. And if I want to look at the trees, I'll do it myself."

The meeting ended with general agreement that it was a nice lunch.

When some people told me what had happened at the luncheon, I laughed and thought, *Finally, someone said no to another good idea. God bless 'em.*

I have a friend who defines a committee as a "group of the incompetent meeting together to do the unnecessary." That is true of some organizations too.

Question Three: *When was the last time you told your pastor (with respect, of course) that you disagreed with something said in the sermon?*

You know what happens. It is a part of the Christian liturgy, which makes the lie OK. The preacher stands at the door as the people come out and say that it was a fine sermon. The preacher replies (again, a part of the Christian liturgy) that he or she is glad that God "used it."

One time I preached a sermon that never made it to the first pew. People were looking at their watches, and then they started shaking them. Then—and nobody knows how hard this is when a sermon has bombed big time—I went to the front door of the church to meet the people and to listen as they told me what a fine sermon it had been.

One teenage girl in the church had just become a Christian, however, and had not been around long enough to learn the "liturgy." She waited to speak to me, leaning against one of the big columns in front of the church. As the teenager listened to the comments of those who filed by, you could see it in her eyes and by the way she cocked her head. She was saying to herself, *Those folks are lying to him. Why are they lying?*

I got more interested in her than in the people who told me how great the bad sermon was, and started wondering what she might say. When they had all filed by and nobody remained to lie, she came over, got on her tiptoes, and kissed me on the cheek. "Pastor," she said, "I love you." Her statement was not altogether different from (though much kinder than) something a friend once told me about a horrible sermon of mine. "Steve," he said, "if I were you, I'd put that one on the bottom of the pile."

Question Four: *Have you ever confronted a Christian leader about a vision or a ministry he or she said came from God?*

The problem with Christian leadership in the church, in media and in denominations, is that these leaders are in danger of having disciples instead of colleagues (or in more religious terms, brothers and sisters in Christ). As a result, some leaders have no one around to tell them when they're doing something stupid. I once told a Christian leader that, if he acted in a certain way, people would think he was a fruitcake. I expected him to get angry; but later he told me he didn't think I really meant it, that I was "speaking in hyperbole."

"Sam (not his name)," I told him, "when I'm speaking in hyperbole, I'll let you know."

If Jim Bakker had had someone around to give the thumbs-down on the water-slide idea; if Oral Roberts had had someone to tell him it was crazy to say that God would kill him if he didn't get a certain amount of money; and if Jimmy Swaggart had had someone to tell him that calling Jim Bakker a "cancer in the Body of Christ" was probably not a good thing to say—a lot of us could have been saved a lot of embarrassment. I use those examples only because they come from leaders we all know. We could add significantly to the list.

A Vote for Honesty

The church is supposed to be the place where honesty is a given. The church is supposed to be the testing place for the people of God where a filter of supernatural love cleanses and purifies—but doesn't eliminate—godly expressions of honesty, criticism, and even harshness. In the church we are supposed to understand the idiocy of worshiping at human, fallible, and silly altars. If we don't understand this when we're with the people of God, then how are we going to be an asset to our culture—the place to which Jesus called us? We are, after all, here for "them." Jesus said, "You are the salt of the earth, but if salt has lost its taste, how shall its saltiness be restored? It is no longer good for anything except to be thrown out and trampled under people's feet."[1]

Something has happened to the Christianity we profess, something that smells like smoke and comes from the pit of hell. We have equated the word *Christian* with the word *proper*, *commitment* with *compromise*, *love* with *sweetness*, *servanthood* with *insipidity*, and *sensitivity* with *banality*.

It is possible, I suppose, that we are simply proper, compromising, sweet, insipid, and banal people, adjusting the Christian faith to conform to our emotional needs. It could be that we have taken the eternal verities of the Bible and made them conform to American cultural standards that make us feel comfortable.

But I don't think so.

I believe that many of us have bought into a neurotic and weak Christianity because we thought it was true Christianity. We have accepted someone else's neurosis as health and have traded in God's freedom for our instinct to pretend and to protect.

Paul, in discussing the difference between law and grace, pointed to the difference between Hagar (the slave) and Sarah (the free). Christians, he said, are not children of bondage. "But what does the Scripture say? Cast out the slave woman and her son, for the son of the slave woman shall not inherit with the son of the free woman. So, brothers, we are not children of the slave but of the free woman. For freedom Christ has set us free; stand firm therefore, and do not submit again to a yoke of slavery."[2] Jesus said that if we obeyed him, he would tell us the truth, and the truth would make us free. And then, as if to put an exclamation on his teaching, Jesus said, "So if the Son sets you free, you will be free indeed."[3]

BOLD AND FREE

Read church history sometime for a reason rather than a grade. You will be surprised.

Irenaeus, during the last quarter of the second century, served as bishop of Lyons. His predecessor, Pothinus, died at the hard hand of Marcus Aurelius. The strength and power of Irenaeus turned almost an entire population to Christ. His most famous work, *Against All Heresies,* boldly defended the Christian faith against all who had challenged it.

Then there was Origen (c. A.D. 185–254) who watched his father, Leonidas, die for his faith in Christ. He stood strong and bold for the rest of his life, only to face torture and finally death at the hands of those who could not abide his courageous strength.

Chrysostom (A.D. 347–407) attacked every social and spiritual evil of his time and for his boldness was exiled, where he died broken in body but not in spirit.

Augustine (A.D. 354–430), a contemporary of Chrysostom, was one of the most earthy Christians Jesus ever called. When told of the fall of Rome, he felt sad but declared while he was a citizen of Rome, he was also a citizen of a city that would never fall . . . a city with a King nobody would ever destroy. His magnificent *City of God* has inspired Christians for centuries.

The sermons of Bernard of Clairvaux (A.D. 1090) ought to be read by every Christian who thinks that *sweet* and *Christian* go together. One biographer of Bernard said of him, "Bernard was a man of humility, but one who spoke with great conviction who, when convinced that he was right, never apologized for his message."[4]

Don't forget Martin Luther, standing at Worms and crying out, "Here I stand. I can do no other, so help me God!"

And then there is John Knox, railing at Queen Mary; the queen crying out in desperation, "I fear the prayers of John Knox more than an army of ten thousand men." You can see in John Knox a passion that many modern-day Christians would find offensive. "Oh, God," he cried, "give me Scotland or I die."

Oh yes, don't forget Peter Cartwright, an early American Methodist pioneer preacher. One story, almost canonical, recalls how U.S. President Andrew Jackson once announced his intention to visit the church where Cartwright was to preach. Certain men who knew Cartwright's fiery tempera-

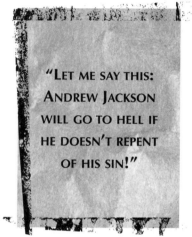

"LET ME SAY THIS: ANDREW JACKSON WILL GO TO HELL IF HE DOESN'T REPENT OF HIS SIN!"

ment pled with him not to offend the president. When Cartwright got up to speak, he began with the following words: "I understand that Andrew Jackson is here this morning. I have been requested to be very guarded in my remarks. Let me say this: Andrew Jackson will go to hell if he doesn't repent of his sin!" After the service, when Jackson met the evangelist at the door, the president is reported to have said, "Sir, if I had a regiment of men like you, I could conquer the world!"

When Cartwright approached a town, it is said he would often stand on a hill above the town and those with him would hear him say, "I smell hell!" Such language! I fear that today we would stand on the same hill and talk about the beautiful flowers and trees that God has made.

The list goes on and on. Gregory, Theodora, Savonarola, Beza, Ridley, Latimer, Zwingli, Wesley, Whitefield, Zinzendorf, the countess of Huntingdon, Newton, Edwards, Mather, and Moody, all sometimes walk in my dreams. There are times when I can almost hear the Scottish Covenanters and the French Huguenots quoting Scripture as they went to their deaths.

CHRISTIANS BECOME COWARDS WHEN WE FORGET . . .

What happened? I suggest that we Christians become cowards when we forget about three important things.

Let's talk about the things we forget.

1. The Truth That Sets Us Free

We Christians do not claim to be part of a group that has voted on what we think is true and has subsequently made that our creed. No! We claim that there is a God who has revealed absolute truth to us, a Holy Spirit who enables us to understand it, and a Messiah who died for it.

It is really foolish to expect others to agree with our truth or to not feel offended when we speak our truth. When something is true, however . . . well, it's true, and you can't change it. Winston Churchill said, "Truth is incontrovertible. Panic may resent it; ignorance may deride it; malice may distort it; but there it is."

I have a friend whose book you ought to read. David Morrison's book *Beyond Gay* chronicles his move from gay, to gay Christian, to just plain Christian. It is written from a Roman Catholic viewpoint, and you will find it informative and helpful.[5]

I met David by mail. I had said something on my broadcast that ticked him off. He was then a practicing homosexual, as well as a regular contributor to a national gay and lesbian newsletter geared to help homosexual Christians feel less isolated.

I don't remember exactly what I said on the broadcast, but his letter brimmed with charges that I had no right to say what I said about him (and others like him), my brothers and sisters in Christ. I don't do "gay bashing," so whatever I said, it wasn't that. I probably said—as I have on numerous occasions—that Christ came to save sinners and that homosexual folks are no exception to sin. I usually state that I'm a sinner too—and not a former one. I generally say, however, that the worst thing about sin isn't the sin; it is calling sin something other than sin.

At any rate, when David wrote that angry letter, I thought about responding in kind. But due to an attack of sanity, I didn't do it. I said that he might well be my brother in Christ and that, given my sin, I was not throwing rocks from my glass house. "The problem, David," I said, "is that when you say something isn't sin when it is, you burn the bridge to God. He can't forgive something you don't think needs forgiving. The Bible says some specific things about your lifestyle and, every time I try to erase it from the Bible, it leaves a smudge on the page."

That was the beginning of a very long series of letters between David and me. We became friends. During that time David started to change. Because of some people who loved him enough to tell him the truth, he began not to change his same sex attraction but to change his views on the nature of that attraction. He became a part of an Episcopal church whose priest, Nicholas Lubefield, remained loving but honest. David made an appointment with the priest.

> I had warned him that this might be a somewhat lengthy meeting and he had done me the service of clearing most of his afternoon schedule. While I sat jumpy as a cat on the large couch, he tilted his head back in the big chair and listened to a condensed version of my life to that point. . . . Through it all Nicholas sat listening, nodding sometimes, occasionally writing something down to jog his memory later.[6]

Nicholas asked some questions of David, ending with this one: "What do you need from me?"

> "Umm, well, I don't know. I guess I just wanted you to know you had a gay activist in your congregation," I said. He nodded and then leaned forward, his serious eyes looking right at me—I have remembered what he said ever since because it had such an enormous impact on my life. "David, if you need me to affirm what you do in bed, I can't, because I think that's sin. But if you need me to affirm you as a brother in Christ, I can do that. Anyone who confesses Christ is welcome here."[7]

One doesn't have to yell when one speaks truth, but one must speak truth. There are so many things that are true that I wish weren't true. I wish two plus two equaled five, because it would mean a significant increase in my bank account. I wish Jesus had said, "It doesn't matter what you believe, so long as you believe something and are sincere about it," because it would save me a lot of criticism. But two plus two isn't five, and Jesus didn't say what I wanted him to say. I wish there were no hell, that all religious people could be right, and that sincerity was more valuable than truth. But there is, they aren't, and it isn't.

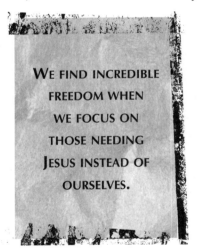

WE FIND INCREDIBLE FREEDOM WHEN WE FOCUS ON THOSE NEEDING JESUS INSTEAD OF OURSELVES.

There is something about truth and being bound by it that will make you bold.

2. The Unsaved

Jesus said, "Behold, I am sending you out as sheep in the midst of wolves, so be wise as serpents and innocent as doves. Beware of men."[8]

The first thing one ought to notice about Jesus' words is that he has sent us out among those "wolves." Second, we are told to remember that we must be careful, because "wolves" are not always benevolent and kind.

But so what? Jesus also said, "All authority in heaven and on earth has been given to me. Go therefore and make disciples of all nations, baptizing them in the name of the Father and of the Son and of the Holy Spirit, teaching them to observe all that I have commanded you. And behold, I am with you always, to the end of the age."[9]

We find incredible freedom when we focus on those needing Jesus instead of ourselves.

So They Might Understand

I confessed to you earlier that I don't have a burden for souls. I'm not proud of it. I do, though, have a burden that those who don't understand will understand. In fact, I'm driven to talk in ways that the unsaved will understand, to communicate in imagery they can grasp, and to take away any barrier to the truth that would prevent them from grasping it. I don't care if they like it. It doesn't matter that they agree with me. I could care less if they think I'm smart, sophisticated, or wonderful. I just want them to understand so they won't ever be able to say that nobody told them.

My friend Ron Minor used to serve as the pastor of a church near Harvard University. Through a weird set of circumstances, Ron got an appointment with one of the professors there. While the professor ran late, Ron waited in his office. Ron told me that, as he looked at the extensive library and thought about this man's reputation and brilliance, he began to feel quite intimidated. Ron did what you and I probably would have done. He thought, *It is important that I not make a fool of myself and bring shame on Christ. I will smile, nod, and keep my mouth shut. I won't speak about anything unless I know something about it. It is better to be thought a fool than to open one's mouth and remove all doubt.*

"*Ron,*" a voice said, "*tell him that Jesus loves him.*"

"Lord," Ron replied, "he'll think I'm silly and superficial."

"*Son, tell him that Jesus loves him.*"

"I can't do that, Father. What would he think?"

The prompting persisted, and before the professor arrived, Ron had decided he would do what he was told. When the professor came into the office, Ron said, "I am here because God sent me here. He told me to tell you that Jesus loves you very much." Then, as simply as Ron knew how, he told this well-known professor the good news about Christ and his love.

Do you know what happened?

Before Ron left that office, the professor's name had been written in the Lamb's Book of Life. Ron's boldness came as a result of God's command, but also as a result of Ron focusing on the professor instead of himself. That kind of thing will make you a tiger—a dangerously free tiger.

Worship Is Also about Us

If you haven't noticed, a great division exists in the church over what is proper and what is not proper in worship.

Some believe in the regulative principle, which states that worship is mandated and prescribed by the Bible. Anything not revealed by God in the Bible should not be used in the worship services of the church. Others think that the church began last Thursday and anything before that is irrelevant. Between those extremes people hold a wide variety of views. Many would die for those views. Someone called this the "worship wars," and that is what it has become.

I'm not going to take a position on the worship wars. I have enough enemies already. Communication is my discipline, not worship. But let me tell you something important to remember. Worship is about God and how he wants to be served and adored. Yet worship is also about us.

No matter how hard you try, you can't force a postmodern rocker to understand and appreciate Handel or Bach, understand a liturgy written two hundred years ago, or think in thought-forms that make no sense to him or her. Through a supernatural love, you can create respect in the family. But people really are wired differently.

Don't forget, I'm making a point about unbelievers. Worship is a public affair, and when pagans wander into the worship services of the church, they should not feel they have moved to another planet. The advice Paul gave about tongues is relevant to this discussion. He said, "And if the bugle gives an indistinct sound, who will get ready for battle? So with yourselves, if with your tongue you utter speech that is not intelligible, how will anyone know what is said? For you will be speaking into the air. . . . If, therefore, the whole church comes together and all speak in tongues, and outsiders or unbelievers enter, will they not say that you are out of your minds?"[10]

Do you want to know something that will make you both free and bold in proclaiming the truth? Desire to be understood, and then take steps to make sure that those who don't know Christ can grasp the reality of what you believe. Perhaps some will come to the truth—and when that happens, you'll discover reservoirs of boldness you never knew existed. And your new freedom will encourage you to take best advantage of them.

3. The Threat

Oops! There isn't one! Once you know there's no threat and your fear disappears, you'll really be free. Since I've already addressed this issue, I won't beat it to death. Still, a word does need to be said here.

Three Courses of Action

When confronted with a threat, most people take one of three courses of action: They *attack, submit,* or *run away.* That is what Christians have been doing.

Some of us, looking at the world, *attack* the unsaved. A lot of our political involvement seems to be of this nature. We see them invading our schools and our political and social institutions, so the culture war and our ability to fight and win become our modus operandi. We need to speak truth and stand clearly for cultural and religious verities, of course, but one would think that our fear drives us instead of our truth. We yell too much, fight too hard, and draw lines in the sand too quickly.

Other times we just *submit.* Some of us have become so enamored with the trinkets of the sellers, so fearful of the swords of the warriors, and so caught up in the harsh bark of the con men, it is hard to tell the difference between us, the sellers of trinkets, the wielders of the swords, and the perpetrators of the cons. In a town where I once pastored, I remember an Episcopal priest's comment as he referred to another pastor who could be seen at the local bar more than in the church pulpit. "He's quit fighting, Steve," my priest friend said. "He's joined them."

And then there are those of us who *flee.* We want to live one-hundred miles away from any known sin. We get into our holy huddles and pretend that the huddle is the only reality. We see no evil, hear no evil, and speak no evil because we fear becoming besotted by the world. We go to Christian movies, associate with Christian friends, eat Christian cookies at Christian restaurants, and wear Christian underwear. Like the science of the mind religionist languishing in hell, we sit in a corner with our eyes closed, saying over and over again to ourselves: "It's not hot and I'm not here. It's not hot and I'm not here. It's not hot . . ."

Stop it! Just stop it!

Pilate must have felt frustrated when, with all of his imperial power, he confronted the bloodied rabbi before him. Pilate held all of the cards, and by all rights, the man who stood in front of him should have begged for mercy. That isn't what happened, however. In fact, one gets the feeling that it was Pilate who was in trouble. "You would have no authority over me at all unless it had been given you from above,"[11] declared the bloodied rabbi.

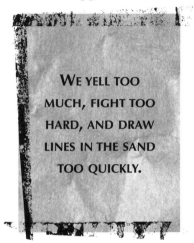

WE YELL TOO MUCH, FIGHT TOO HARD, AND DRAW LINES IN THE SAND TOO QUICKLY.

Earlier Jesus had said, "What I tell you in the dark, say in the light, and what you hear whispered, proclaim on the housetops. And do not fear those who kill the body but cannot kill the soul. Rather fear him who can destroy both soul and body in hell." And then, just as a reminder, Jesus added, "Are not two sparrows sold for a penny? And not one of them will fall to the ground apart from your Father. But even the hairs of your head are all numbered. Fear not, therefore; you are of more value than many sparrows."[12]

If this is true, what threat should have the power to make us afraid?

A Fourth Course

I once heard a professor give a lecture to a gathering of students and colleagues. His opening remarks assured that no one would fall asleep during his address.

"Seeing as how the board," he said, smiling, "has seen fit not to renew my contract, there are some things I've been meaning to say." He then got out a verbal howitzer and proceeded to shoot at everybody and everything that had anything to do with his soon-to-be-former employer.

Had I asked him where he found the courage and the freedom to say such things, he would have said, "What are they going to do to me? Fire me?"

This is the course of action that should be adopted by Christians. Instead of attacking, submitting, or fleeing, they should ask *what are they going to do*? Are they going to take away my stuff? It's not mine. It's God's, and you can't take from me what isn't mine. I have a friend who drives a Mercedes. Right after he became a Christian, he had some major engine trouble, and the car quit working on the way to his office. He got out, looked at the car, and said, "Lord, look what's happened to your car."

What are they going to do? Take away my reputation? I don't boast of one, and the one I have isn't all that good. As I understand it, Christians are folks who came to the astounding truth that we're not very good people, but God is fond of us anyway.

A young man once got angry at something I said. I didn't want to hear his retort because I feared it would be spiritual nonsense. I finally said to him, "OK, son. If you want to be honest, I'll listen to what you have to say."

"Dr. Brown, I think you are arrogant, rude, and prideful."

"You're right," I responded. "But I'm better than I was."

What are they going to do? Manipulate me with guilt? Fat chance. I remember the comment of the lady who, twenty years prior, had been unfaithful to her husband. Finally she decided to confess it to him. Her husband told her he had always known and forgave her from the beginning. When I saw her, she was dancing like a little girl. "He had already forgiven me! I'm free!"

What are they going to do? Kill me? Doesn't matter. I was going to die anyway, and being a Christian martyr isn't all that bad. As someone has said, "I don't think I'm good enough to be a saint, but I could be a martyr if they killed me fast." Some major long-term benefits have been set aside for me after I'm dead.

What are they going to do? Take away their love? I get more critical letters than you could possibly imagine. After I read them, I think, *I have a wife who loves me, a family who accepts me, some friends who don't think it's permanent when I've made a fool of myself. And even more important than all of those, I have a God who will never be angry at me again.* I am loved by those who will never take away their love. I don't care if you don't love me.

Paul answers the question of whether anything can separate us from Christ. He writes: "No, in all these things we are more than conquerors through him who loved us. For I am sure that neither death nor life, nor angels nor rulers, nor things present nor things to come, nor powers, nor height nor depth, nor anything else in all creation, will be able to separate us from the love of God in Christ Jesus our Lord."[13]

Just what are they going to do? They have no leverage. And without leverage, they have no power.

Some bemoan the present state of things. "We've lost our power and our influence," they say. "We are no longer respected in the community. No longer are our preacher's sermons published in the newspapers of our towns and cities. We can't threaten the politicians with the loss of our vote," they whine, "because their constituency is now with the doubters and the pagans."

A cultural agreement about what is right and wrong no longer exists. A prophetic voice so often seems irrelevant. No longer do we get preferred treatment from the leaders, respect from the world, or fair treatment in the media. We are the brunt of their jokes, the object of their scorn, and the target of their false characterizations.

That's bad.

No, that's good.

Now we have to do it Jesus' way. Real boldness is just another name for nothing left to lose. And Christians who have nothing left to lose are the world's worst nightmare!

A FEW SUGGESTIONS

Before we wrap this up, let me make some suggestions that are doable only if you understand the freedom that is yours. I'm not into spiritual steps to anything. Mostly, when I try them, I find some of the stairs have gone missing, and I end up back down in the basement. Nevertheless, let me suggest that you follow these simple steps.

- First, offend someone for the right reason.

- Second, don't apologize for the wrong reasons.

- Third, accept the result of offending and not apologizing.

- Finally, take those three steps to Jesus, and you will discover something important. He will say: "Child, been there, done that, and have the T-shirt."

Well, maybe he won't say it quite that way, but he will understand. Why? Because there is a price to be paid for not being liked. And he has paid it.

Oh, and don't forget the product you get when you pay the price:

Their respect . . .

your freedom . . .

and his pleasure.

For we know that the whole creation has been groaning together in the pains of childbirth until now.

—Romans 8:22

CHAPTER
NINE

THE PAIN WE AVOID . . .
and the Reality That Sets Us Free

NO MAN CAN BE BRAVE WHO THINKS PAIN THE GREATEST EVIL;
NOR TEMPERATE, WHO CONSIDERS PLEASURE THE HIGHEST GOOD.
—CICERO

"The tendency to avoid problems and the emotional suffering inherent in them," M. Scott Peck has written, "is the primary basis of all human mental illness."[1] Carl Jung has written, "Neurosis is always a substitute for legitimate suffering."[2] My friend Larry Crabb says we all have a place of pain and that we try to go any-place but there. He says that, in order to get to a place of wholeness, we have to keep on probing and probing at the pain until it gets so bad only God can fix it.

I don't always agree with Dr. Peck, hardly ever agree with Jung, and almost always agree with Dr. Crabb. But when you get those three saying essentially the same thing, you probably ought to pay attention. That is what we're going to do in this chapter as we look at how we lose freedom in our eagerness to avoid pain. In fact, if you understood that first paragraph, you've got the point. What follows is simply commentary.

WE CAN'T AVOID PAIN

I don't know where in the world we got the idea that, if we're Christians, we can avoid pain—emotional, physical, and psychological pain. It isn't as if God ever told us such a thing. The Bible is quite clear on the subject.

Christians are often like the cat that gets its tail caught in a crack and tries to figure out how to get it out without getting hurt. That cat can't do it, and neither can you. Frankly, it is unbiblical and counterproductive to your freedom to think you're going to get out of this thing without it hurting—and sometimes really bad pain.

We get thousands of questions at Key Life, and a great number of them concern the problem of emotional and physical suffering. Here's a sampling:

> "I've been depressed for months. My doctor said that I ought to be on some medication, but I told him I was a Christian and that God would make it better. He hasn't. What do I do?"

> "They told me at church that if I had faith my daughter would get well. I guess I don't have enough faith because she is worse. Is it really a matter of faith?"

> "My friends say that Christians shouldn't have emotional problems because we have God. Is that true?"

> "Isn't God for marriage? My husband just left me for another woman. I've prayed and prayed, and he still left. If it is God's will for my marriage to be a good one, what am I doing wrong?"

> "My mother just died of cancer. I don't think I believe in God anymore. How could he allow her death?"

> "I struggle with addiction to pornography and don't have any place to turn. I'm doubting my salvation and the power of God to help me. I've prayed about it, but it doesn't help. Do you think I'm a Christian?"

> "My boy is on drugs, and I just found out. I don't know what his

mother and I have done wrong. We have been a Christian family and have taught our children Christian values. And now this. Can you help me understand?"

I suspect that you have had your own questions. I know I have.

Years ago I was asked to give a lecture on Pauline theology at a local community college. I suppose it was part of an effort by a worldly institution to be fair to the "weird religious folks." It was a fun time—they always are—because it gives me an opportunity to shatter some unfortunate stereotypes. After I finished the lecture, the professor and I were talking, and she began to cry. I asked her if I could help. It turned out that she was a fairly new Christian and had unfortunately gotten involved with some dear folks whose hearts had found Jesus but whose heads had not yet quite made it.

She told me those Christians had informed her that if she had enough faith and exercised the right principles, her small child, who had juvenile diabetes, would get well. That was silly enough, but what she told me next was not only silly—it was dangerous. They told her she had to demonstrate her faith by stopping the regular insulin injections. If she did that, they counseled her, then God would honor her faith and heal her child.

What an impossible situation! If she stopped the insulin and her child died, she would have been responsible. If she continued the insulin and her child's disease continued, then that would have been her fault too. The comments of her Christian friends were, at best, highly presumptuous.

I felt thankful that I was able to tell her the truth. Her friends were sincere, but wrong. I wondered, as I walked away from that small college, how much damage had been done by sincere Christians with really unbiblical ideas. I wondered how many others didn't have anyone to speak the truth to them.

I don't want you to be one of them.

THE TRUTH ABOUT PAIN

Not understanding the truth about pain will put you in a horrible prison of guilt and anger and rob you of your freedom. So pay attention while I tell you what the Bible really says about emotional and physical suffering.

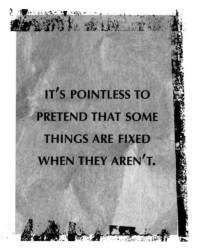

IT'S POINTLESS TO PRETEND THAT SOME THINGS ARE FIXED WHEN THEY AREN'T.

Some Things Aren't Fixed

You and I never met him, but he messed it up for the rest of us. His name was Adam. He and his wife, Eve, did some really bad things for which they were cursed. Bad thing for us is that they were the first of our race, and what happened to them affected the rest of us.

God said to Eve, "I will surely multiply your pain in childbearing; in pain you shall bring forth children."[3] While Eve reeled from that bit of revelation, God said to Adam, "Cursed is the ground because of you; in pain you shall eat of it all the days of your life; thorns and thistles it shall bring forth for you; and you shall eat the plants of the field. By the sweat of your face you shall eat bread, till you return to the ground, for out of it you were taken; for you are dust, and to dust you shall return."[4]

In other words, "Men must work and women must weep, and the sooner it's over, the sooner to sleep."

It's been mostly downhill since then.

Well, at least until Jesus came. The Bible calls him the "second Adam," and a lot of the stuff the first one messed up the second One fixed. But that's another book. This chapter is about the things that weren't fixed and won't be until we get to heaven and about how freeing it is to know. This chapter is also about how pointless it is to pretend that some things are fixed when they aren't.

The Bible tells us plainly about some things that aren't fixed.

> For I consider that the sufferings of this present time are not worth comparing with the glory that is to be revealed to us. For the creation waits with eager longing for the revealing of the sons of God. For the creation was subjected to futility, not willingly, but because of him who subjected it, in hope that the creation itself will be set free from its bondage to decay and obtain the freedom of the glory of the children of God. For we know that the whole creation has been groaning together in the pains of childbirth until now. And not only the creation, but we ourselves, who have the firstfruits of the Spirit, groan inwardly as we wait eagerly for adoption as sons, the redemption of our bodies.[5]

While there is some good news in that passage of Scripture, there are also some incontrovertible and unpleasant realities that we ignore at our own peril. The passage says we have suffering in "this present time," as well as "futility," "bondage of corruption," "groaning," and "pangs."

I'm going to get to the good news about freedom, but good news isn't really good news until you first know, understand, and accept the bad news.

Life Is Not Easy

I have never understood how Christians who claim to follow the One who ended up hanging spread-eagle on the town garbage heap between two thieves could ever come up with the crazy ideas that life is easy, that we won't suffer, and that God's primary purpose in the world is to make us happy and to give us the good life.

In fact, Jesus made his views quite clear on the subject. "In the world," he said, "you will have tribulation."[6] He told his followers that they would be persecuted and hated: "If the world hates you, know that it has hated me before it hated you. . . . Remember the word that I said to you: 'A servant is not greater than his master.' If they persecuted me, they will also persecute you."[7]

Paul talks about the fellowship of Jesus' suffering[8] and sometimes even rejoices in his own suffering.[9] When God called Paul to serve Christ, Jesus said he was going to show Paul how much he must suffer.[10] At one point Paul seems quite proud of his suffering.[11] And believe it or not, Paul even puts believing in Jesus and suffering for him on the same plane, using a form of the word *grace* to describe both.[12]

Jeremiah the prophet felt so down he wanted to give up;[13] Paul felt so depressed he despaired of life itself;[14] Peter feared others and their opinion of him;[15] sickness dogged the experience of the early church;[16] and what can we say about Job's experience with pain, loss, and rejection?

Did you hear about the young man who visited the fortune teller? She looked at his palm, read his tarot cards, and said, "Young man, you are going to be miserable, broke, and lonely until you are forty years of age."

"Good heavens," he exclaimed. "What will happen after that?"

"Then," she said, "you'll get used to it."

I'm not suggesting that things are bad and you're just going to have to get used to it. God is still God, he still answers prayer, he is still moved with compassion, and he still intervenes and changes circumstances.

God Sometimes Grants Healing

I once served as a pastor of a church where every quarter we did something not generally done in Presbyterian churches. I prayed about it, however, and felt God's leading in that direction. I broached the idea with the elders of the church, and we agreed—

some of us with significant questions—to proceed with a prayer/healing service.

Once we made the decision for the elders to publicly pray for and anoint with oil those who requested prayer, I had a problem. Well, actually two problems.

First, we were Presbyterian, and Presbyterians aren't Charismatics. Charismatic Christians, you might know, believe that God still acts in supernatural ways, that he is involved with his people, and that he answers prayers. They have a tendency to be rather free, loud, and open in their worship services, often speaking in tongues, dancing, and expressing themselves with words of praise. We Presbyterians don't raise our hands above our belts; we do not say anything not contained in the order of worship; and if you praise God aloud apart from the liturgy, then you will be told that you "simply can't do that in here." So I explained to the congregation that we were going to have prayer services in the context of Holy Communion, and that it would be done decently, in order, and quietly.

That was when I noticed Patti in her wheelchair, in her regular, reserved place close to the front. Patti had found Christ through a tragic suicide attempt that had put her in a wheelchair for life. She would smile and say she would rather be in a wheelchair and know Christ than to be whole and never have known him. As I looked at her, I stopped my proper Presbyterian comments and said, "However, if Patti gets out of that wheelchair, I *will* speak in tongues and dance!"

The second problem was more serious. So, to protect and prepare my people, I detest presumption—especially the claim that God always heals, blesses, and answers our prayers in the affirmative. I had taught (sometimes, I fear, rather harshly) that Christians should learn to deal with suffering and pain. I said the Christian faith was not power without pressure, but power under pressure.

I had taught the theme so often that I found it hard to convince my people that God sometimes did say yes, that prayers sometimes do effectively change circumstances, and that we worshiped a supernatural God who, when it matched his loving plan, acted in a supernatural way on behalf of his people.

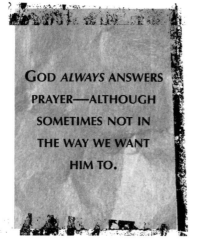

GOD *ALWAYS* ANSWERS PRAYER—ALTHOUGH SOMETIMES NOT IN THE WAY WE WANT HIM TO.

I didn't want them to misunderstand, and I don't want you to misunderstand what I'm about to say either. God *does* answer prayer. In fact, he *always* answers prayer—although sometimes not in the way we want him to. God is God, and he does as he pleases. God likes us a lot, and he enjoys saying yes. Our daughter, Jennifer, was healed in a supernatural way because some Anglican Charismatic Christians prayed for her. (By the way, that's why I don't make fun of Charismatics in electrical storms.)

The Bible says, "For all the promises of God find their Yes in him. That is why it is through him that we utter our Amen to God for his glory."[17]

Christians Don't Get a Pass

During my years as a young pastor, I was speaking for a group of churches in the hills of Tennessee when I got the message that my father was dying. No one I loved had ever died before, and I started crying. One pastor hugged me and said, "Son, use this. Every time you speak to ten people, seven of them will have a broken heart."

As we've already established, being a Christian does not make you an outsider of the human race. When you stick a Christian with a pin, he or she will bleed. If a Christian has been traumatized as a child, there is a good chance that the Christian will pay an emotional price for the trauma. Christians get cancer, they feel depressed, and they die. The death statistic is still one out of one.

Saint Teresa of Avila, the Spanish contemplative of the sixteenth century, prayed the way many of us would if we were more honest and free. She prayed: "Lord, you would have more friends if you treated the ones you had a little better." But, in fact, in terms of pain—the pain endemic and pandemic to the human race—Christians don't get a pass. Sometimes it gets bad . . . really bad.

WHAT HAPPENS WHEN WE TRY TO AVOID PAIN

The point isn't that we, as Christians, have it bad. The point is that we get ourselves into trouble when we think we don't have it bad, when we try to avoid having it bad, or when we pretend that it isn't bad. If you don't acknowledge your problem, you can't fix it. If you pretend you don't have a problem, you can't fix anybody else's problem. And if you believe that you shouldn't have a problem, you will kill yourself with guilt over your problem.

Let's talk about three results of trying to avoid pain.

1. We Lose Our Freedom to Be Honest

Trying to avoid pain (which you can't do anyway) will dilute the quality of your life and take away your freedom to be honest, to discover God's faithfulness, and to rejoice in the courage that he has given. Believe me, I know.

A Cape Cod Incident

When I was a young pastor on Cape Cod, the doctors told me about an elderly lady who lay dying. That was their job. But they went beyond their job in telling me that she simply couldn't deal with the emotional trauma of her impending death. They told me this lady read books only with happy endings, avoided any negative talk about almost any subject, and liked to live in a world in which everything looked rosy and wonderful.

"She just can't bear," the doctors said to this very young and naive pastor, "the emotional shock of facing a terminal disease."

That presented them with a problem, however, and they asked me for help. They said the lady needed nursing care, but the nurses wouldn't work if they didn't think they would be paid. (Dead people don't write checks.) The doctors told me they needed to get this dying lady to sign a power-of-attorney form, but they had to get her to do it *without* telling her the truth about her imminent demise.

I am not proud of what I did, but I complied with their request. I held this lady up in her bed and guided her hand as she signed a form she could barely see. I was young then and didn't know what I know now. Even so, I remember feeling guilty that I had somehow betrayed the woman who deserved much better. She required honesty, and I had given her lies. She required someone to hold her and to walk with her through the valley of death, yet I had stood there on the sidelines, telling her that the valley wasn't there. She required a pastor to talk to her about eternal things, and I talked to her about trivial things. She needed the freedom only the truth will give, and I robbed her of that freedom by taking the truth from her.

I'm a lot older now and a little bit wiser. After that incident I decided two things that have become cornerstones of my life and ministry: First, doctors are not God, and half the time—especially in the healing of souls—they generally don't know what they are doing. Second, I decided I would never again lie that way . . . ever. People need their pastor to help them face the pain, not to lie to them about its existence.

Do Not Be Surprised

Jesus said to his disciples that he had some bad news for them and some good news. The bad news, he said, was that they were going to have tribulations and that people would hate them. Then he gave them the good news: He had overcome the world, so in the end, it would be OK.

Peter said to Christians, "In this you rejoice, though now for a little while, if necessary, you have been grieved by various trials, so that the tested genuineness of your faith—more precious than gold that perishes though it is tested by fire—may be found to result in praise and glory and honor at the revelation of Jesus Christ."[18] In the same letter, apparently to address the very human proclivity to deny the reality of pain, Peter wrote, "Beloved, do not be surprised at the fiery trial when it comes upon you to test you, as though something strange were happening to you."[19]

Let me give you a principle: *There is a direct correlation between your willingness to face the darkness of your own pain and your ability to live freely and fully.*

I had my first serious automobile accident while in college. I worked for a radio station and was driving across the mountains to my home when I ran off the road, skidded, and totaled the car in a tumble down the side of the mountain. (I woke up unconscious, several feet from the demolished car, and had no idea how I got there. At that moment I figured God might have something more for me than spinning records as a disk jockey.) I was devastated for a number of reasons. First and most important, it was my first car; I loved that car more than any since. I also realized that everyone would know how stupid I had been.

But I also felt quite fearful about ever driving a car again.

The next day my very wise father made me get in his car and

drive it. I didn't want to. The last thing I wanted to do was to get in something that I had so recently discovered could be so dangerous. But he made me do it. "Son," he said, "if you don't start driving again soon, you will remain afraid. You have to face the source of your fear and conquer it."

My dad was right about driving. But more than that, his wise words apply equally well to life in general.

Kiss the Demon

Are you afraid of death? "No," you say, "I'm a Christian. I may be a little anxious, I might sometimes think about it and wonder, and there are a few times when I'm not so sure I'd want to die anytime soon."

THE DEMON WON'T
GO AWAY UNLESS
YOU FACE IT.

Balderdash!

That's called fear. So let me give you some advice on facing death, and then apply that advice to a whole bunch of other unpleasant and painful areas.

Anybody who says the thought of their own death doesn't scare them will lie about other things. ("The good news is that you're going to heaven. The bad news is going on Thursday.") *But if you don't face it, you will always fear it. And that very fear will keep you from the freedom in which God would have you live.*

The next time you think about your own death, determine to look that demon straight in the eyes. Think about your funeral, the casket where your corpse will rest, and the people who will grieve or rejoice (as the case may be). Sometimes Spurgeon, the famous preacher, would fall asleep while picturing himself in his coffin.

That may sound a little weird, but, in fact, it was quite wise. Why? Because the demon won't go away unless you face it.

It is important that you face the reality of your own death until you just can't do it anymore. Then go and do something else (watch television or go to a movie). But before you look away, say to the demon of fear, *I'm not through with you, buster. I'll be back.*

Then, after you rest up for a bit (sometimes the resting time is days), go back to the place of your fear and repeat the process. Then do it again. Eventually, you will be able to think about death—*your* death—with a degree of peace and acceptance. After that, you will be able to live your life with incredible freedom.

Now, take this principle and apply it to every area of fear, pain, and anxiety you have. It will surprise you at how freeing it is to kiss the demon on the lips. The demon loses its power over you, and you can get on about the business of really living.

A Quiet Flight

It happened a number of years ago on a flight from Miami to Los Angeles. We were all enjoying a happy trip, since most of the passengers were returning from cruises. They had their trinkets in their hands, tans on their faces, and great memories to share when they returned home.

And then the lady in the aisle next to my seat died.

Everybody got real quiet while the flight attendants asked if there were a doctor on the flight. Two or three came forward, and while they did their best to save her, she still died.

The pilot landed the plane in Dallas and directed his passengers to disembark while the corpse was taken from the plane to a waiting hearse. Then we all reboarded the plane for the remainder of our flight to Los Angeles.

The crowd had changed into a somber bunch. Most people try to avoid death and all thoughts of it. But to be honest, it is hard to do that while encased in an aluminum tube cruising at 34,000 feet. There just isn't anyplace to run.

I approached one of the flight attendants. "I'm a clergyman," I said, "and deal with death a lot. If you would like me to help, please feel free to ask."

"Thanks for your offer, Reverend," she said, smiling, "but we're going to give the passengers free drinks."

Can you believe that? If you can get them drunk enough, they won't have to deal with the reality of death. Just souse 'em up.

I fear that Christians sometimes do that too. Only we don't use alcohol; we use religious clichés, false theology, and Christian denial.

Don't do it. It will rob you of living free. You have to face pain before you will ever be free of it. It's really unwise to look away from the reality of pain, because then you never risk and you never live. There are a lot of dead people walking around who have yet to be buried.

Kiss the Demon, Take Two

Are you afraid of cancer, your wife leaving, or your son or daughter leaving the Christian faith? Do you stay awake at night thinking about what would happen if you lost your job or had an accident that disabled you for life or killed you? Are you sometimes fearful that people will discover something bad you've done? Do you wonder how you would handle it if you lost your stuff, had to file for bankruptcy, and became homeless? Do you ever think that everybody could reject you, that you could become an outcast and have to live in loneliness forever?

Maybe some of those things already have happened and you

fear that you won't make it through. Perhaps you think you've reached your limit and you're afraid that you can't take much more. Just name your demon.

Let me give you a prayer to pray. You don't have to use these words, but try something like them: *Father, I'm scared . . . really scared. I have this horrible fear of _____, and I can't get rid of it. Grant me your peace and allow me to remember that you are God, that you are in charge of the circumstances of my life, and that you will never leave me or forsake me. Remind me of your love and your power, and give me whatever I need to deal with my fear of _____.*

The Bible says that God "gave us a spirit not of fear but of power and love and self-control."[20]

There is horrible bondage in pretending that the world is a nice place, that bad things really don't happen to Christians, and that God will put a permanent hedge around you. That kind of denial makes you even more afraid, because truth has a way of haunting our darkness.

Face it. Admit it. Struggle with it. Kiss the demon on the lips. Lift it to God, and you will begin—not, perhaps, quickly or easily—to experience an incredible freedom that the demon tried to take away.

2. Our View of Reality Is Disfigured

Someone has said that a neurotic is a person who builds fantasy houses, a psychotic is someone who builds fantasy houses and lives in them, and a psychiatrist is someone who charges rent.

Christians shouldn't live in fantasy houses. By looking away from the reality of pain and suffering in the world, we create a world that doesn't exist and then try to live in it. But the last person in the world who ought to be unrealistic about anything should be a Christian.

Chapter Nine

Only Missionaries Allowed

I love missionaries . . . but not when they're home.

I know that isn't a particularly kind thing to say, but I'm trying to be honest here. When missionaries are home, they're generally raising money (deputation work), and they have to be nice. The men will generally shave their beards, smile a lot, and say the right words. The women take off their jeans, don a dress, put on makeup, and become quite proper and religious.

But if you want to really know missionaries, you have to go where they serve. You have to get down with them in the dirt and in the grime of their "place." You would like them better there. They have dirt under their fingernails and steel in their backbones. They are earthy, real, and practical. I've visited a lot of mission works around the world and remember my visits as some of the best times of my life.

I once spoke for a mission conference at which the church members had a wisdom far beyond their own. Let me tell you about it.

The church had invited some twenty-five missionaries, in addition to myself and a couple of other speakers. For the better part of a week, the missionaries presented their work to the congregation, explaining the way God was working and asking for prayer (and, of course, money). When I noticed a missionary luncheon on the schedule, I commented to one leader that the church seemed to be working the missionaries to death. I said I thought it a bit much.

She laughed and said, "You are quite right, but you don't understand. This isn't your ordinary mission luncheon. This is a lunch for missionaries, which only missionaries are allowed to attend."

She then explained how the people of the church fixed lunch (a great one, by the way) and then just left the missionaries alone. "We thought," she said, "they must be tired of the show, that they needed a place to be themselves, to say what they wanted to say, and to be real. So, we prayed about it and decided to give them that opportunity."

Is that great or what?

The missionaries invited me to be a part of their lunch; it was like fresh air. The missionaries didn't just talk about the people who had found Christ, but also about those they had lost. They talked about their doubts as well as their faith. They talked about both success and failure. They rejoiced in God's healing of their pain, but they also commiserated with one another about the pain God had chosen not to heal.

For a whole week, I lived on their vulnerability, honesty, and openness. But I felt sad too, because the church had to create a special place where that kind of reality could be expressed. That should not have been necessary. In fact, every place where Christians are should be a place filled with honesty and reality.

> THEY HAD FREEDOM THAT COMES FROM FACING THE WORST AND DEALING WITH IT.

Do you know the thing that felt most wonderful about that missionary luncheon? The incredible freedom! A freedom that can come only from people who have looked at the world the way it really is . . . with all of its pain, its loss, and its uncertainties. They had freedom that comes from facing the worst and dealing with it. I saw tears that day. But let me tell you what else I saw: I saw laughter, joy, and freedom.

Don't Look Away

When Jesus declared that he intended to send us into a dangerous world, he also said that we were to be "wise as a serpents."[21] Among other things, that means Christians should never look away from reality, pretend that things are different from what they are, or ride the horses of wishes. ("If wishes were horses, beggars would ride.")

Too often we Christians lose our freedom by taking the clear promises of Scripture, meant to apply to heaven, and trying to force those future promises into some unauthentic, present application. God will someday "wipe away every tear" from our eyes. Someday there will be no more "mourning nor crying nor pain."[22] But that time is not yet—and it is sheer lunacy to pretend that it is. It will drive you crazy and rob you of your freedom.

But the problem doesn't stop there. When you start lying to yourself about the pain, you begin to fudge on everything else. The church becomes a fantasyland rivaling anything Disney ever created. Throughout history it has been the Christians who cleaned up the messes of the world. When a plague hit, it was the Christians who nursed the sick and buried the dead. The pagans ran because they couldn't face the reality.

Our family has a heritage of facing reality and doing something about it. We have educated the ignorant, adopted the orphans, fed the hungry, and emptied the bedpans of the sick. When we stop doing that because the reality is too . . . well, real, we have betrayed something important about God's call on our lives.

3. The Truths That Set Us Free Are Distorted

I'm not in the business of throwing rocks at belief systems different from mine. As I stated, when we get home, I think all of us will find out that we erred in some important areas.

Two Views

Some in the church follow the teachings of the Word of Faith movement. As I understand it, those folks believe that if you speak it properly and with the right amount of faith, it happens.

On the other end of the spectrum, some Reformed brethren among us believe that no matter how much faith you have, how often you speak it, pray for it, and look for it to happen, it probably never will . . . and if it does, you'll probably miss it. So deal with it.

I consider both views heretical. The Word of Faith movement is wrong, but so are the Reformed people. Both are presumptuous, although in different directions. One believes that God *always* says yes, and the other believes that God *never* says yes.

Let me suggest that any system of doctrine that makes God into a magician who banishes bad things is false. In other words, when you twist Scripture and try to force it into a mold that ignores the reality of evil, it cuts at the heart of biblical theology. Biblical Christianity is about truth that sets the believer free. The Bible takes evil very seriously. When we try to ignore what the Bible says by repeating the twenty-third Psalm over and over again, we become shallow and ineffective.

Did you hear about the ugly American who approached a Third World Christian sitting serenely under a palm tree?

"What are you reading?" the American asked.

"The Bible."

"In my country that book is out of date."

"If it were out of date here, you would have been eaten by now."

The Bible is a balanced book that takes seriously our sin and the pain we suffer. When we try to make the Bible endorse a life of denial, the power of truth gets lost and Christians sound silly. And everybody knows it.

Silliness will make you feel better for the short haul, but reality has a way of breaking through and smacking us upside the head with a two-by-four. The freest people in the world are Christians who know that the world is not a nice place where "God is in his heaven and all is right." They know about the Fall, about pain, about sin, and about danger. In the knowing, they find wonderful freedom. It says, "I'm called to be here and to even suffer sometimes, but I'll face the reality and dance anyway."

Now that's being free.

4. We Deprive Ourselves of God's Grace and Sufficiency

The twenty-third Psalm is good news, but don't miss its message. "Even though I walk through the valley of the shadow of death, Thou art with me." If you won't go there, if you won't face its darkness and its pain, if you play games with evil and call it anything but evil, you will never experience the sufficiency of Christ. And you'll miss out on large chunks of grace that could have been yours.

Paul's Thorn in the Flesh

You'll find one of the most powerful passages in the entire Bible in 2 Corinthians 12. The Holy Spirit reminds the apostle Paul that he can't escape pain.

Paul calls his problem a "thorn in the flesh," and nobody can say for sure what it was. It was probably some kind of physical malady, but could perhaps be something else. Whatever it was, Paul pleaded with God to remove it. I suspect Paul said some things to God that we have all said numerous times:

- "Lord, this thing is destroying me. I can't survive if you don't do something else."

- "Lord, I would like to be whole, like others. This thing really hurts my witness, and there are people who say that if I had enough faith, it would disappear. Would you do something about it?"

- "Lord, if you healed me, I would give you the credit, maybe even write a book with my testimony in it. Lord, think of the great honor and glory it would bring to you."

But listen to what God said to Paul: "My grace is sufficient for you, for my power is made perfect in weakness."[23] In other words, "Paul, if you didn't have the wound, you wouldn't have the power."

If you could grant your children freedom from pain, problems, and hardships, would you?

WHENEVER AN UNBELIEVER AND A CHRISTIAN GET CANCER, THE WORLD SHOULD BE ABLE TO SEE THE DIFFERENCE IN HOW THEY HANDLE IT.

Don't be so fast with your answer. Think about it. Many successful people work hard so their children won't have to go through what they went through. "What they went through," however, is exactly what made them successful and great.

Whenever an unbeliever and a Christian gets cancer the world should be able to see the difference in how they handle it. When a pagan and a christian go through a marriage problems, the world gets the chance to see how christians handle marriage problems. When a pagan and a Christian lose a business, face death, suffers the pain of loss, the world can see the difference that Christ makes.

So when you hurt, don't run from the pain. Embrace it. Run to it, not away from it. It has shown up so that you will find God—and sometimes that is the only place you can find him.

As a preacher acquaintance of mine once said, "People are always saying, 'Jesus is all I need.' But you won't know Jesus is all you need until Jesus is all you have. When Jesus is all you have, then, and only then, will you know that Jesus is all you need."

From an Inch to a Mile

Have you ever noticed that people who have everything are sometimes silly and superficial? We all know the prettiest girl in class who is also vacuous, the star athlete who missed the question about two plus two, or the bright young executive who can't hold down a job.

It is insane to lend credence to the political and social views of most movie stars and wealthy philanthropists because, with some significant exceptions, they simply haven't lived long enough or hurt deeply enough to have much worthwhile to say.

Buddy Greene, the recording artist, told me once that he asked God to increase the sales of his recordings and the size of the crowds at his concerts.

"Do you know what God told me?" he asked me.

I didn't.

"He told me," Buddy said, grinning, "that if he gave me an inch, I would take a mile."

And speaking of Buddy, he has a song on a CD about broken roads. The song declares that every broken road leads to God. If you refuse to walk on the broken roads, pretend they aren't broken, or believe there aren't any broken roads, you'll never get to him. If you turn away from the pain, pretend it doesn't exist, or get upset and angry because of the pain, you will never know God's wonderful sufficiency and grace.

Let your broken roads lead you to God, and there you will find an incredible freedom and joy. The Bible says,

> But when one turns to the Lord, the veil is removed. Now the Lord is the Spirit, and where the Spirit of the Lord is, there is freedom. And we all, with unveiled face, beholding the glory of the Lord, are being transformed into the same image from one degree of glory to another. For this comes from the Lord, who is the Spirit.[24]

But There's More

My wife and I survived Hurricane Andrew in South Florida. If you remember, Andrew ranked as one of the most devastating natural disasters in U.S. history. When the hurricane hit, we were holed up in our house and had done everything we could to prepare.

It wasn't nearly enough.

The hurricane slammed into Florida with far more force than anybody expected. As we crouched in the bedroom closet, we became aware of the very real possibility that we might die. We listened in horror as trees crashed into our home, the roof blew off, and our house fell apart.

That was really bad, but there's more.

After we lost much of our stuff in the hurricane, we got another surprise. A dishonest contractor stole some $60,000, and other contractors put $15,000 in liens on our home. That was $75,000 we didn't have.

That was really bad, but there's more.

When I went out to the parking lot of the small apartment where we stayed in the interim, I found that someone had stolen our car.

That was really bad, but there's more.

Shortly after the hurricane, the doctor informed us that my mother didn't have long to live. We had no place to bring her (we no longer had a house), so we went to the old homestead in the mountains of North Carolina to nurse my mother until her death. I took a small recorder and prepared the daily broadcast from the back porch of my mother's home and handled most of the business and ministry of Key Life by fax and phone.

Most of my life has been fairly easy. Up to that point, I had never faced devastating tragedy. I always wondered how I would handle it if something really bad happened. I would sometimes preach on pain and suffering, knowing that my words had a hollow ring because I was talking about something distant from my own experience.

It was a horrible experience. But it was wonderful too. My Christian mother faced her death with profound peace. She said good-bye to her friends and family, gave her grandchildren advice, prayed a lot, and told jokes. Can you believe that? My wife and I laughed at her jokes and even told some of our own.

Oh yes, there were tears, pain, and fear.

But in the middle of all this tragedy, God came. And in facing it all, we discovered a boundless and exhilarating freedom and joy we had never known.

It wasn't the freedom of the Christian who pretends that things are all right when they're not. It was the freedom that only believers who have faced pain and tragedy know. It was the freedom of Jesus who, when we've lost it all, invites us to laugh, dance, and sing in his presence, knowing that nothing will ever separate us from him and his love. It was the freedom of knowing that he is more important than anything else.

Pain is not something most people like. That is why we run from it as fast as we can. That is also why we aren't free. Jesus hardly ever goes to those places where we run.

When pain comes (or when we fear that it will come), don't run away. Run to it, and you will find you have run into the arms of Jesus. In other words, buck up, face it, embrace it, and know that you and Jesus can deal with it.

Then you will laugh and dance in the freedom and the reality of God's sufficiency and the power that becomes awesome in your weakness.

FOR I KNOW THE PLANS I HAVE FOR YOU, DECLARES THE
LORD, PLANS FOR WHOLENESS AND NOT FOR EVIL, TO
GIVE YOU A FUTURE AND A HOPE.

—JEREMIAH 29:11

CHAPTER
TEN

THE FAILURE WE FOSTER . . .
and the Victory That Sets Us Free

HE HAS ACHIEVED SUCCESS WHO HAS LIVED WELL,
LAUGHED OFTEN, AND LOVED MUCH.
—BESSIE ANDERSON STANLEY

"I'm a failure," she wrote, "and it has been good for me to be a failure. I've learned so much from my mistakes, and God has allowed me to see him in a far different and more profound way than I did before. Thank you for your prayers. I praise God that he is in charge of every circumstance."

I felt glad for what she had learned. I rejoiced with her about the new ways she had discovered God. I gave thanks that she was "still trucking" and, of course, I affirmed her belief in God's sovereignty.

Something, however, seemed a little off about her letter, so I called her. Do you know what I discovered? I discovered she had failed because she had set herself up for failure and had used Jesus to justify it. I wanted to tell her (but didn't) what she should have learned from her mistakes—she had made some very bad decisions, had ignored some sound advice, and had refused some gracious help. Then she had given God the "credit" for her failure.

My friend Fred Smith has said that the difference between Christians and pagans when both fail is that pagans blame luck and Christians blame God. Unfortunately, there is some truth in that.

But let me tell you about some other truth. Many Christians live in a prison of failure, thinking they cannot gain their freedom from that prison. They aren't free because they think they don't deserve freedom. They have lived in the abnormality of a dark prison for so long they won't look up at the open door God has given them—an open door into the light of freedom.

Do Christians fail? Of course they do!

A rampant "cult" of failure among Christians, however, can kill off our freedom. Let's talk about it.

TINTED EMOTIONAL GLASSES

Most bad theology is bad psychology. A neurotic person will probably choose to believe some neurotic things about God and religion. A mean person will find a reason to be mean in his or her theological commitments, and a Pollyanna person will probably have a Pollyanna belief system. We see truth through our own emotional glasses, and that makes it very hard to separate the true from the tainted.

Too often an angry pagan will become an angry Christian, a pagan with a bad self-image will be a Christian with a bad self-image, and a defeated pagan will become a defeated Christian. That is sad, because we really are (or should be) a "new creation. The old has passed away; behold, the new has come."[1]

Let me suggest the problem. The truth is that if you are a Christian, you became one because you were lacking, in need, and a sinner. We all came to Christ because we knew we desperately needed to be forgiven, to change, and to become different.

Motivated by Guilt

A number of years ago I participated in a study by a Harvard doctoral student whose dissertation concerned why people went into religious professions. He had designed a questionnaire to measure the motivations of ministers, priests, and rabbis for choosing a religious vocation.

I don't remember the exact statistics, but I do remember they revealed a phenomenally high common motivation: A significant majority of us were motivated by guilt. We felt terribly guilty and thought we could assuage the guilt, or make up for what we perceived as a serious deficiency in our lives, by becoming "full-time" Christian or Jewish professionals.

In our Born Free seminar, we teach that guilty people make people feel guilty, and you can tell how guilty a person really is by perceiving how guilty you feel in his or her presence. Given that truth and the general motivation of why people go into ministry, I often tell my students that God didn't check with me about how he got them to seminary; but if they don't deal with their guilt, they will end up having a ministry of condemnation. And I remind them of what Paul wrote: "There is therefore now no condemnation for those who are in Christ Jesus."[2]

I fear too often the church has become an organization of guilty people with a guilty preacher standing in the pulpit, telling guilty people that they should feel guiltier.

I'm surprised that any of us ever accomplish anything of note in the name of Christ. Potential lions get defanged, potential heroes and heroines get cut off at the knees, and potential winners become losers.

I don't think Christ went to the trouble he did in order for us to become feeble and ineffectual Christians who sit in the corner, whining about how horrible we are.

Do you?

No Need to Wince

In this chapter I want to share something about the law of God.

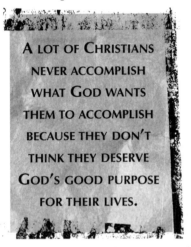

A LOT OF CHRISTIANS NEVER ACCOMPLISH WHAT GOD WANTS THEM TO ACCOMPLISH BECAUSE THEY DON'T THINK THEY DESERVE GOD'S GOOD PURPOSE FOR THEIR LIVES.

This isn't going to be as bad as you think. Trust me on this. In fact, the reason you winced when I mentioned the law of God is because you (and I) have misused it, have felt driven by it, and have been condemned by it.

But that isn't the purpose of the law.

I believe a lot of Christians never accomplish what God wants them to accomplish because they don't think they deserve God's good purpose for their lives. Christians often see themselves as bound and helpless sinners, deserving of any punishment an angry God might choose to dish out. A part of that, of course, is true. We don't deserve anything commendable. We haven't earned anything good. We can never be good enough, pure enough, or strong enough to earn God's grace. That much is true—but it isn't the whole truth. Not by a long shot.

I once had a German shepherd whose previous owner had beaten him. His name was Calvin, and he was one big, strong dog. He just didn't know it. I gave him the name Calvin because I thought it would help him with his extremely bad self-image. It didn't. In fact, I've never seen a dog expect punishment more than Calvin. It wasn't that he had done anything wrong; it was just that he had somehow gotten the idea he was a bad dog and that my sole purpose in life was to beat up on him because he was such a bad dog.

No, I never hit Calvin. I didn't even raise my voice to him. I praised him, petted him, scratched behind his ears, gave him treats, and did everything I knew to foster a good self-image. Nevertheless, Calvin flinched every time I came near him.

Do you know what happened? He became the bad dog he thought he was. German shepherds are supposed to protect and defend their owners—Calvin ran and hid under the bed. German shepherds are supposed to lie at their master's feet—Calvin wouldn't come near me. German shepherds are supposed to be strong and courageous—Calvin was a weenie. I really believe Calvin felt sort of uncomfortable and abnormal because I didn't do what he expected me to do—punish him.

RETHINKING TWO WORDS

Before we get too far into this, let me pause to define two words often used in a pejorative and improper sense among Christians.

The first word I want to define is *success*. By success, I don't mean that you become the president of your company, get voted the most popular person in your class, become famous, make lots of money, or get asked by every service club in your town to give a talk titled "Success and How I Attained It." My definition of success doesn't preclude that sort of thing, but it focuses on something else entirely: becoming all God would have you to be. By success, I mean the kind of life not held back by some kind of imagined restraint from a God who has decided that, if anything good happens to you, he made a mistake.

Consider the faulty reasoning that enslaves many Christians:

Major premise: Christians are undeserving sinners.

Minor premise: I'm an undeserving sinner.

Conclusion: I deserve nothing but failure.

While there is some truth to such logic, it is only a part of the story and, believe it or not, a very small part. I have a friend, Pete Hammond, who got a card from his daughter on his sixtieth birthday that read, "Hey, Dad. In spite of all those conflicts, scenes, and anxious moments, you're turning out just fine." Well, despite your sin, your unworthiness, and your rebellion, you're going to turn out fine—unless you decide not to turn out fine. Does that surprise you? It does me, and I fear the reason it does is because I have misunderstood the gospel. Such a serious misunderstanding is one of the major reasons we aren't free to be all God would have us to be.

Humility is the second word we need to talk about. Did you hear about the man whose club gave him a medal for being the most humble man in the club but then took it away because he wore it? We're sort of like that in the church.

We are enormously valuable, so valuable that God would buy us at the highest price ever given for any object. He sent his Son. We are to be free, excited, and even proud (in the best sense of that word) of our salvation and his love. But what happens if any of us shows the slightest indication of our true value? Someone will admonish us for not being humble.

I don't know about you, but I'm tired of it.

Paul didn't particularly care for false humility: "Do not let anyone who delights in *false humility* and the worship of angels disqualify you."[3] Thereupon follows a list of religious stuff that can kill Christians. Then, to make sure that his friends got the point, Paul continued, "Such regulations indeed have an appearance of wisdom, with their self-imposed worship, their *false humility* and their harsh treatment of the body, but they lack any value in restraining sensual indulgence."[4]

Humility is not dishonesty. It does not baptize your inferiority complex, turning it into a Christian asset. Neither does humility deny God's grace in your life. Humility is simply knowing who you are and feeling comfortable with it. Humility is never lying to yourself about your gifts, the knowledge you have acquired, or the value God has said you have or don't have. Humility is always measuring yourself by the Infinite. It is not standing next to your fellow Christians and determining your comparative worth. When you're good, it is saying so. When you do something right, it is knowing you did it right. When you shine, it is knowing you shine. And then humility means giving all of those flowers and bouquets back to the God who gave them to you.

Now let's talk about the law and its relationship to the horrible prison of failure we foster. God would have you free of that.

GOLD, HONEY, AND REWARDS

It is important to understand that the law of God is . . . well, the law of God.

God doesn't make suggestions. The psalmist writes, "The law of the LORD is perfect, reviving the soul; the testimony of the LORD is sure, making wise the simple; the precepts of the LORD are right, rejoicing the heart; the commandment of the LORD is pure, enlightening the eyes." Then the psalmist says, "More to be desired are they than gold, even much fine gold; sweeter also than honey and drippings of the honeycomb. Moreover, by them is your servant warned; in keeping them there is great reward."[5]

That passage almost always surprises Christians. We don't have any trouble with the first part about the law being perfect; it's the "gold," "honey," and "reward" part that we don't understand. Do you know why? Because we have come to see the law of God as a negative thing given by a negative God to negative people who will never get it right. We either nullify the law by saying it no longer applies to Christians who "don't live under the law, but under grace," or we give the law a condemning power God never intended. In either case we get in trouble.

Let me show you a better way—the biblical way.

A FABULOUS GIFT

Our Jewish friends know a secret: The law of God is one of the very best gifts God ever gave them. There are several reasons for that.

First, the law of God provides a schematic for the way the world works. God didn't sit around trying to think up things we might enjoy and then make a law prohibiting them. Rather, because he saw no percentage in keeping his people in the dark, he told us how things really work. When the psalmist says the law makes the simple wise, he means God explains how certain things will hurt you and certain things will help you. What a gift to know the difference!

God doesn't say, "I hate sex; it's dirty. I know how much you enjoy it, therefore, I hereby declare that adultery is sin." Rather, God says, "If you want to really mess up your life, be miserable, and pay a price you don't want to pay, then commit adultery. It will do all of that to you and to everybody you love."

God doesn't tell us to be honest because he thinks it will cause us to lose business. He tells us to be honest because honesty really is the best policy.

Covetousness isn't God's great plan to keep us in our place so those in power can stay in theirs. He tells us not to covet because he knows that true peace comes, not in getting what you want, but in wanting what you have.

If you aren't a believer and want to know how to have as much happiness as possible in the world, you don't have to be religious, go to church, or believe stuff you can't believe. All you have to do is to follow the law of God, insofar as you can follow it. To the degree you do so, you will be happy. It is no big secret. The law of God, as revealed in the Bible, is the best way to live. Not only will you be happier living by it, but if you teach it to others, they won't steal your car.

Second, the law of God is a safeguard. When you walk in a minefield, you might want to know the location of the mines. The positive side of the law brings happiness, while the negative side provides protection. One will make you feel better, and the other will keep you from getting killed. It has been said so often that it has become a cliché, but you really don't break the law of God; you break yourself against the law of God.

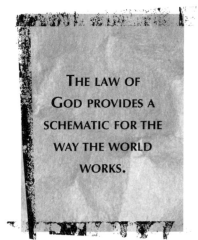

THE LAW OF GOD PROVIDES A SCHEMATIC FOR THE WAY THE WORLD WORKS.

Third, the law of God is a sampler. Utopian schemes, whether they come from the Christian right or the Communist left, generally injure those who have to suffer under them. They start by throwing the scoundrels out, but end by putting worse scoundrels in. When the end justifies the means, the end becomes too horrible to contemplate. I'm not antistatist (against the state) because I lack compassion. I'm antistatist because do-gooders are dangerous, especially when they wield great power. God save me from politicians, Christians, or pagans who think they are my mother!

Even with all of that being said, however, it is no accident that the laws of Western civilization are based on the revealed laws of

God in the Bible. Those laws point to a just, compassionate, benevolent society, and to the extent a society codifies those laws and does a reasonably proficient job of living by them, that society will echo the way things get done in heaven. When Jesus said that we ought to pray, "Thy will be done on earth as it is in heaven," he meant that we ought to pray for the laws of heaven to be lived out on earth. Things would be a whole lot better if that were to happen.

The concepts that the law is a schematic, a safeguard, and a sampler are true in a general and universal sense. I could preach that sermon at the Rotary Club and "that dog would hunt." Unbelievers may not like the sermon; but it remains true nevertheless, and the smart ones know it. If I were an atheist, reasonably intelligent, and had even a modicum of concern for my community and my country, I would still preach that sermon.

So what does all of this have to do with freedom in general and success in particular? Stay with me. I'm getting there.

For the most part, what I just told you can help everyone—pagans, Buddhists, atheists, New Age folk, and everyone else. What follows, however, applies only to believers in Christ.

A Wonderful Tutor

Would you like to hear some dynamite news about the law of God? Paul says, "So then, the law was our guardian until Christ came, in order that we might be justified by faith."[6] (The Greek word for *guardian* implies teacher or tutor.) Do you know what the law did for you? In the struggle to keep it, you realized you were in trouble; and unless you know you're in trouble when you really are in trouble, you're in *real serious* trouble.

The law is the tutor that brings you to Christ.

When he entered my office, I had the feeling I would never see him again. The look on his face suggested he didn't want to be there and wouldn't stay very long. I had been his friend for almost two years; during that time I had tried to witness to him. The problem? He didn't think he needed Christ. And in a purely human sense, he was one of the best men I've ever known. He was a good and faithful husband, a caring and wise father, a good citizen involved in the community, and a benevolent employer admired by his employees. He had money, served as the president of a number of professional organizations, and took an active role in the leadership of our local service club. He came to church, not necessarily because he believed in it, but because good people went to church; besides, it seemed good for his family and the community.

As soon as the door closed, however, he started crying. He didn't want to, but he couldn't help it. He then confessed to a horrible—and what was soon to become public—sin. He felt appalled not only at what he had done; he felt horrified at the public shame it would bring to his family and himself.

"Steve," he said, "I'm so ashamed. After I tell you what I have to tell you, if you don't want me as a part of the church or if you want me to just leave you alone, I will understand."

"Good heavens, man," I replied. "I can't imagine what you could tell me that would cause me to want you to leave the church or leave me alone unless, of course, you're gay and are ready to make a pass at me. And even if that were true, we would still be friends with a couple of ground rules."

I intended my poor effort at humor to put him at ease. It didn't. He proceeded with his confession. I will spare you the details, but you do need to know his confession deeply pained both of us.

"Jack (not his name)," I said softly, "I'm so glad this has happened. If it had not happened, you would have lived your entire life believing you didn't need Christ. Now, finally, you don't have any angles to play. The thing you need right now is forgiveness and grace. And the only one who can give you enough to get you through this is Jesus."

For the first time in the two years I had known him, he listened and understood the good news of the gospel. I wish he could have listened and understood without having to go through the pain, but hardly anyone ever does. That's bad. No, that's good, because

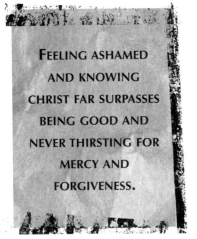

FEELING ASHAMED AND KNOWING CHRIST FAR SURPASSES BEING GOOD AND NEVER THIRSTING FOR MERCY AND FORGIVENESS.

through the pain of self-revelation, exposed by the law, we come to the throne of grace. The most dangerous thing in Jack's case was not his sin, *but his thinking that he had no sin*—or at least, no sin needing the sacrifice of Christ.

If you are reading this because you count yourself a good person and good people read religious books, let me give you a warning: You are dancing on the edge of a cliff. One day, maybe soon, you're going to fall off. Not only that, but when you fall off, it's going to hurt really bad. I just wanted you to know, and I didn't want you to say that nobody ever told you. I just told you.

By the way, let me tell you what happened to Jack. He later told me that, while he hated that awful time, it was the best thing that had ever happened to him. Why? Because feeling ashamed and knowing Christ far surpasses being good and never thirsting for mercy and forgiveness.

I'm honestly glad he went through it. I never liked him much before. He was pompous and arrogant, and the more he tried to hide his arrogance, the worse it became. He's a lot easier to live with now.

An Amazing Glue

The law not only acts as the tutor that brings us to Christ; it also functions as the glue that keeps us there.

The apostle Paul gives his testimony in Romans 7 about the state of his life. (Some suggest Paul talks here about his past experience, but the last time I checked, both Paul and God knew about verb tenses. If Paul had been describing his experience in the past, where the statute of limitations had run out, he would have said so.) Paul said that when he wanted to do good things, he couldn't; and when he didn't want to do bad things, he couldn't help it. Paul called it an ongoing problem in his life. And he bellows the cry of agony that every believer knows: "Wretched man that I am! Who will deliver me from this body of death?" And then the wonderful answer: "Thanks be to God through Jesus Christ our Lord!"[7]

At some point we come to the end of ourselves, and that happens quite often. Given the situation Paul describes here—and he was a better person than I am and probably better than you too—our sin and failure cause us time and again to run to Jesus. We cry out with Paul, "I'm in trouble here. Can anybody help?"

And Jesus says, "I can. I can help."

How does he help?

First, when we go to God, he accepts us no matter how dirty we are. I can't tell you the number of times I have crept into the throne room of God thinking, *He's going to really get me this time. I'm history. He will never accept me this time because I've been here like this so often.* It always surprises me—but it really shouldn't, given what the Bible says—to hear him say, "Come here, child. I was wondering when you would come. I was waiting."

Do you know what I feel when I leave God's presence? I feel really good . . . no, not good in the moral sense. I *feel* good. I also feel so incredibly grateful that I can hardly contain it. In fact, when I go through that experience, I want to tell everyone about him. "Hey," I want to shout, "he's not angry at me! He's not angry at all. How about that? Can you believe it? If you go to God, he won't be angry at you either."

Love in response to goodness isn't love, but reward. Fortunately for us, that's not God's way. Our relationship with God is not a matter of reward, but of love. And that's why we can enjoy such staggering freedom in his presence.

Second, when we go to God, sometimes he begins to change us and to make us different than we were before we went to him. But you'll get into trouble if you make this an absolute. If you believe that every time you confess sin (pointed out by the law) to God, then he automatically gives you the power to obey, you'll believe anything. Sometimes God will change us, and sometimes he won't.

The revelation of your sin—as painful as that is—is a gift from God. Do you remember Jack, the man who confessed to me? After he became a Christian, I found him a lot easier to live with. The arrogance had disappeared, and he became delightfully human. But if you think I told you Jack's story to tell you that, after he sinned, he became a wonderful, obedient, and perfect Christian, you would be wrong. That didn't happen. I think he was better, but he still struggled. And for Jack, that wasn't even the point. God's grace was the point.

HE GIVES HIMSELF

Thomas Kelly, a Quaker and one of the most profound and insightful contemplatives of the twentieth century, said in a lecture he gave in 1938:

> The old self, the little self—how weak it is, and how absurdly confident and how absurdly timid it has been! How jealously we

guard its strange, precious pride! Famished for superiority-feeling, as Alfred Adler pointed out, its defeats must be offset by a dole of petty victories. In religious matters we still thought that we should struggle to present to God a suitable offering of service. We planned, we prayed, we suffered, we carried the burden. The we, the self, how subtly it intrudes itself into religion![8]

Sometimes God will give us the gift of obedience, and sometimes he won't. When God doesn't, he gives us love and forgiveness. But more important than that, God gives us himself—freely, joyously, and without reservation.

And when he does give us the gift of obedience, God also gives us an acute awareness that it wasn't us; it was him. We had very little to do with the obedience except, of course, that we went to him. And even that came by his bidding and through his grace.

It becomes a win/win proposition. You get to feel better, you will sometimes be better, God will be glorified (after all, that's why we're here), and God's plan for us and for the world will shine.

If you've been a Christian very long, you may be wondering why I left out the guilt, the condemnation, and the promises to get better and better in every way, every day. I left them out because they simply aren't in the Bible. I am drawn to that stuff too, but it simply isn't there.

If you use the law of God to condemn yourself, go ahead, but don't say it's from God. If you allow others to use the law to make you guilty and afraid, go ahead, but don't call them God's servants. If you use the law to judge others, go ahead, but don't assume that your judgment mimics the judgment of God. If you use the law to make you feel superior to other Christians and pagans, you can do that too, but please remember God didn't give you the law for that purpose. You aren't superior or better, not even a little.

So deal with it.

THE WAY TO SUCCESS

Let's talk about success in the way I defined it at the beginning of this chapter.

Something about religion will, if you let it, make you into an insecure, self-doubting, failure-producing worm.

It happens with the misuse of the law. When we get involved in religion, the encounter of the finite with the Infinite will produce a significant sense of inferiority. Enough rules, regulations, and laws exist in every religion (including ours) to kill off any hope you have of ever measuring up. You can allow the rules, the regulations, and the laws to create a humble habit (a false one) that will destroy you and what God will have for you.

In other words, you can define yourself—listen up, this is important!—by your inevitable failure to live up to the standards, or you can define yourself in terms of God's love, acceptance, and the great value he has put on you.

Let me tell you about me. I have always wanted to pastor a megachurch. In fact, all my life I've thought about it, dreamed about it, and savored the possibility.

It has never happened.

I regularly speak in churches where they have more staff than I have members and where the choirs are bigger than any congregation I ever served as pastor. I've pleaded with God for a big church. I've told God that I would be good if he would just grant my request.

He never did.

Or, at least, I thought he never did.

Occasionally I got offered a big church, but something always went wrong. For instance, I interviewed with one church with an arrogance and pride that, even as I tell you about it now, makes me blush. The former pastor had stayed there for almost twenty-five years, and I knew that, if I didn't present a strong image and if I weren't strong (should the church call me), I would end up being a sacrificial lamb. So I was strong. Boy, was I strong!

During the interview they asked what I would change if they should call me to be their pastor. I told them that I would change almost everything.

"When I walked through the sanctuary," I said, "I heard your organist. The first thing I would do is to fire her. Not only that, I would require that every member of the staff submit his or her resignation to me the day I became the pastor."

> YOU CAN DEFINE YOURSELF BY YOUR INEVITABLE FAILURE TO LIVE UP TO THE STANDARDS, OR YOU CAN DEFINE YOURSELF IN TERMS OF GOD'S LOVE.

"Anything else?" asked one of the members of the pulpit committee.

"Oh yes. I visited the bookstore you guys have downtown and looked over some of the titles. A lot of the books you carry are heresy, and I would burn about half of them."

Needless to say, the interview ended with everyone acting civil and nice, but it became quite clear that it would be cold in a hot place before they ever called me as their pastor. Pastors are supposed to be reasonably kind and compassionate; I showed none of that, whatsoever. Later, my friend Leighton Ford who had submitted my name to the committee, called and said, "Steve, they're going to call someone else. They said that you were a bit much for them."

I felt good about the whole process. I had been my own man. I had stood for truth, justice, and the American way. If they couldn't understand that, then they deserved what they got for a pastor.

And then God started working on me. It was a very painful

experience. He pointed out my arrogance, my pride, and my horrible attitude. I thought he told me, "No wonder I don't give you a big church. You would have messed it up the way you've messed up other things."

I now understand that the words I thought were from God actually came from *me*! It was my own self-condemning psyche speaking. It happened because I had misused the law. I blew the interview because I felt (deeper than I knew at the time) that I was unworthy, sinful, and inferior. My unconscionable actions before that pulpit committee served as my portable foxhole whereby I could say, "I remained faithful to God and showed great strength, but they didn't want me." It was far easier to say that than to say, "I am a failure, and I don't need to fail in a church that big."

Do you see it? We all have feelings of inferiority, some because we really are inferior and some not based on reality at all. But it was our inferiority that brought us to Christ in the first place! Once those feelings bring us to that point, they fulfill their purpose.

If you don't learn to deal with guilt properly and biblically, it serves no purpose.

A Logic Correction

Remember the line of faulty reasoning I showed you earlier in this chapter? Let me bring it back and correct it:

Major premise: Christians are undeserving sinners, and I'm an undeserving sinner.

Minor premise: God's grace is bigger than my sin, and his love is bigger than my failure.

Conclusion: Therefore, I gratefully accept any blessing he deems proper for me.

If we don't take special care, an improper use of the law will confirm our inferiority, if that is our inclination, and if it isn't, it will give us that inclination. When that happens Satan will rejoice, and you will become as useless as you have come to think you are. When the law gets preached, taught, and believed without the preaching, teaching, and understanding that God has given us the law as a gift; then the freedom God would have for us—and the success that comes from that freedom—will go wanting.

Speaking of success, isn't Tiger Woods something else? If I had not given up golf years ago, just watching him would make me burn my golf clubs. Nobody should be that good and that successful.

I came across a great magazine article the other day that discussed the reasons for Tiger's outsized success. You have to hear what Woods's father, Earl, said: "If you stay angry with yourself for a bad shot, you won't be able to prepare for the next one. Tiger can get real angry with himself for a bad shot, but he doesn't let that affect him for the next one. That's the key: Play every shot with the same frame of mind and let go of what happened before."[9]

That really is the key. One must live life in the present and, ultimately, only a Christian can do that. It is our heritage of freedom. The past is the past, forgiven and redeemed; the future is ours, a gift our Father will give us. God has put us in the present as a place to struggle, succeed (or fail), risk, and make a difference.

The difference between a slingshot as a kid's toy and a slingshot as a mighty weapon to slay giants is found in the hands of the one who holds the slingshot and the One who gave it. Give a slingshot to a struggling, failing, and inferior Christian with a faulty "humble habit," and that Christian can shoot only at cans. Give it to a free, forgiven, loved, and valuable child of the King, and that Christian can kill a giant.

What's that in your hand?

Who gave it to you?

What did he tell you to do with it?

CHAPTER TEN

HOW GREEN DO YOU WANT IT?

On a trip to Ireland, the actor Richard Harris rented a car with a stick shift. Being famous and rich, he had always driven cars with automatic shifts, or he traveled in a car driven by someone else.

After Harris drove the car out of the rental lot, he stopped for a red light, and the car promptly died on him. When the light turned green, he started the engine again and tried to change gears and get moving, but he just couldn't get it into gear. The more he tried, the less progress he made. Meanwhile, the light turned back to red and then to green several times.

Finally, an Irishman in the car behind him sauntered up to Harris's car. "Excuse me for askin'," the man said to Harris, "but was it a particular shade of green you were waitin' for?"

You're free . . . really free. You're free because you are forgiven and loved. God is for you and controls all the circumstances of your life.

So get moving.

Was it a particular shade of green you were waiting for?

For freedom Christ has set us free; stand firm therefore, and do not submit again to a yoke of slavery.

—Galatians 5:1

CHAPTER
ELEVEN

THE PATH WE AVOID . . .
and the Journey That Sets Us Free

GOD HAS LAID UPON MAN THE DUTY OF BEING FREE, OF
SAFEGUARDING FREEDOM OF SPIRIT, NO MATTER HOW DIFFICULT THAT
MAY BE OR HOW MUCH SACRIFICE AND SUFFERING IT MAY REQUIRE.
—NIKOLAI BERDYAEV

I have a friend who says he is so spontaneous he's going to write a book on it: *Spontaneity and the Ten Steps to Attaining It.* That title doesn't work, because once you follow the steps to spontaneity, you've lost the very thing you set out to attain. Spontaneity is . . . well, spontaneous.

Just so, something about freedom gets lost when one starts obeying certain rules in order to attain it. Forget about ten steps to freedom. Nobody can tell you that if you do certain things, you will be free. If someone (other than Jesus) tells you that you will be free only if you do what he or she says, you're being lied to.

That is the reason I almost didn't write this final chapter. I didn't want to take away your freedom by telling you how to get it. I didn't want to create another twelve-step program so you can get busy doing the very thing that binds Christians. I didn't want to create a manual for freedom so that you could reference it to see how you're doing with your commitment to freedom.

I love doing Born Free seminars around the country. But I some-times feel uncomfortable teaching them because we all want a guru to tell us what to do, how to do it, and what it will look like when we've done it. As I've said, all my life I've looked for wise Christians I could follow, but every time I found one, they shattered my image and kicked down the very altar I had constructed. I guess that sometimes I still look for gurus. I'm learning that only Jesus can do the guru thing; however, you might be surprised at how rarely he plays that role.

A radio pastor used to do an evening show during which he answered questions from listeners. One night a little boy called and asked if his deceased dog would be in heaven. "Son," the man replied, "I don't know. But when you get there, whistle and see if he comes."

Something in me wants to say to you (and to myself) that we just ought to be free—live free, speak with freedom, offend those who don't understand freedom, test it, walk in it, proclaim it—and see if Jesus makes it real to you. I believe he will, but I do think a little more needs to be said. So, I'm going to say it—but be careful with what fol-lows. I'm not the guru. I'm just a pointer, pointing to the One who, by his very presence, is himself the freedom he gives to his own.

One last thing, and then we'll get started. I once wrote a book that never got published. I had titled it *The Ten Stupid Things Christians Do to Mess Up Their Lives*. The publisher didn't like the word *stupid* and suggested that I title it *The Ten Dumb Things Christians Do to Mess Up Their Lives*. My son-in-law laughed and said that the book could end up being titled *Some Inappropriate Things Christians Do to Mess Up Their Lives*. The book wasn't very good, and it's probably best it was never published. This chapter, however, is going to be a bit like my son-in-law's joke. I should probably call this chapter *Some Suggestions You Might Find Helpful*, because what follows are just some suggestions.

THE RIGHT TEACHER

I've been snow skiing only once, and I did that in the Swiss Alps. My wife and I were staying with some Swiss friends who literally grew up on skis. They went shopping on skis, headed to the movies on skis, and left for church on skis. Their skis had become a part of them. They forgot that some people do not feel comfortable on skis. They just assumed everybody grew up knowing how to ski, just the way people grow up knowing how to breathe.

That is the only explanation I have for their putting me on a major ski slope without a single lesson. They didn't even tell me how to stop. As their guest, I figured they knew what was best and started down the slope. I quickly realized I was going faster than human beings are supposed to go without an airplane. While I did figure out how to stop, I didn't do so the way I wanted to. Hitting trees can be quite unpleasant while traveling as fast as I was.

That was when I started doing serious prayer. Among other things, I told the Lord that if he got me down alive, I would never do this again. He did and I haven't.

But should I ever foolishly decide to try it again, I'm going to look for the right teacher: someone who has tried and failed several times. I want a teacher who has broken his or her leg at least once. I don't want a teacher who thinks that skiing is easy. I want someone who knows that people die on ski slopes and who has had some degree of pain in learning.

I've been walking with Jesus for a long time, and no doubt I've done it wrong more than I've done it right. There is something to be said, however, for listening to someone who struggles mightily with being free. If you want someone who has been there, done that, and has the T-shirt to prove it, then I'm your man. Don't take me too seriously, but don't ignore what I'm going to tell you either. I've

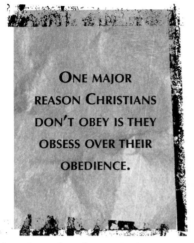

ONE MAJOR REASON CHRISTIANS DON'T OBEY IS THEY OBSESS OVER THEIR OBEDIENCE.

gone down (and sometimes still try to go down) several paths that I would spare you.

Bound by Efforts to Be Free

Peter said, "Live as people who are free, not using your freedom as a cover-up for evil."[1] Paul said essentially the same thing. In his great work on freedom, Galatians, he said, "For you were called to freedom, brothers. Only do not use your freedom as an opportunity for the flesh, but through love serve one another."[2]

I am not a confrontational person. I don't like to confront people about anything. In fact, when I was a pastor, my ministry philosophy (before Jesus changed it) was, "I'll leave you alone if you leave me alone." I like to be liked, and if you confront people too much, they grow to dislike you. I've always known I avoided confrontation, and I've always known I was wrong.

That is the reason, believe it or not, I have a reputation for being in-your-face confrontational. I live in fear of being a weenie, of compromising and selling my soul to get along. So, when I was a pastor, I made a rule that, at least once a month, I would confront someone about something. Do you know what happened? I hurt a lot of people by my confrontation. I felt so afraid of not confronting people that I confronted them too much.

Freedom is like that. Some people who have discovered the reality of freedom don't want to go back to prison. That is good—but if you aren't careful, you can create another prison just as horrible and just as dark as the prison from which you escaped. It's like little boys who smoke or look at *Playboy* out behind the barn because . . . well, because they are free and they can. They don't understand they can get addicted to both.

Paul said, "'All things are lawful for me,' but not all things are helpful. 'All things are lawful for me,' but I will not be enslaved by anything."[3] In other words, you are really free—but don't be stupid about it. Don't get bound by your use of freedom.

Will God still love you if you use your freedom for license or, in the exercise of your freedom, you do something harmful to yourself or to others? Of course he will—but you be careful out there.

So Obsessed We Lose It

Paul said he prayed for the Christians in Ephesus that:

> According to the riches of his glory he may grant you to be strengthened with power through his Spirit in your inner being, so that Christ may dwell in your heart through faith—that you, being rooted and grounded in love, may have strength to comprehend with all the saints what is the breadth and length and height and depth, and to know the love of Christ that surpasses knowledge, that you may be filled with all the fullness of God.[4]

If I've tried to do anything in this book, it has been to get you and myself away from obsessing over our sin. The rules are so hard, and there are so many of them. If you get obsessive over rules and laws, you will end up breaking them all. In fact, one major reason Christians don't obey is they obsess over their obedience.

Let it go, and quit making your goodness the issue! This isn't about you and me; it's about Jesus. When you obsess over anything but him—and that includes being free—you can lose it. Jesus *is* freedom, and to the degree you stay focused on him, you will find yourself free.

If you don't obsess over Jesus, will he still love you? Of course he will—but you be careful out there.

Afraid and Running

Paul wrote to Timothy that God has not given us a spirit of fear;[5] the psalmist said that God delivers us from our fears;[6] Isaiah said that we don't need to be afraid because God is our strength and our song;[7] and John said that the more we are loved, the less we fear, and there is no fear in love.[8]

That all sounds so good, but can we talk?

I've too often felt so afraid of freedom that, while I knew it was there, I ran from it. Most of us feel afraid, and our fears, more often than not, have to do with things not so apparent.

We fear that we will blow it really bad—so bad we can't fix it. We fear losing control and doing something stupid. We fear what others think. We have obeyed and bowed before those who have manipulated us for so long, it scares us to change. We have fallen into patterns of actions that, while they may have caused us pain, are still our patterns, and we fear to change them. What will other Christians think? What if I jump off this cliff to freedom, trust God and risk, and get killed? We go on and on.

Almost anything you do with God that comes from fear is probably wrong. So be afraid, but be free too, and then you won't be so afraid. We teach an important principle in the Born Free seminar: *You take the first step, God will take the second step, and by the time you get to the third step, you will know that it was God who took the first step.*

Will God love you if you let your fear keep you bound? Of course he will, but you will miss the joy of laughing and dancing in his presence. He does not want you to miss that. It's really fun. So, you be careful out there.

Bound by Our Past

The Bible says a lot about how our past can affect our future. Peter made a wonderful statement about past and present. He said, "You are a chosen race, a royal priesthood, a holy nation, a people for his own possession, that you may proclaim the excellencies of him who called you out of darkness into his marvelous light. Once you were not a people, but now you are God's people; once you had not received mercy, but now you have received mercy."[9]

In other words, your past is your past. You may have to revisit it in order to understand the abuse, the dishonor, and the way you have been disvalued. You may have to go there with Jesus; sometimes that isn't easy, and it takes a long time. But Jesus will go with you. And when you come back, learn to identify your prisons through his light and not through the darkness of your past.

I've sometimes been bound, not because I didn't understand the wonderful gift of freedom, but because of my past. Maybe you have too.

I have a friend I love. She has done some really destructive and shameful things. One time when we were talking, she took out a worn picture of herself taken when she was a little girl. She said, through the tears, "Steve, sometimes I look at that picture and I say to myself, 'What have I done to that little girl?'"

She didn't do anything to that little girl, but a whole lot of other people did. She needed to go back, to maybe get angry, to maybe analyze her past, and to understand it. Then, having gone there, she could be free. The past can take away your freedom. So, you be careful out there.

Letting Others Define Us

Jesus called us his "friends" and offered us unconditional love.[10] Jesus called himself our elder brother.[11] God highly values us and has adopted us into his family.[12] That is our reality, and that is how God wants us to define ourselves.

The angry people around you will get even angrier if you are free. Don't listen to them. Listen to Jesus. "He himself is our peace."[13]

If you listen to them and don't think well of yourself, will God still love you? Oh yes. Of course he will—but you be careful out there.

We Shilly-Shally

Paul said, "For freedom Christ has set us free; stand firm therefore, and do not submit again to the yoke of slavery."[14]

I once spoke at a conference at which the other plenary speaker and I had a question-and-answer session. One question came from a young man who said, "I have been quite disturbed by some of the things Dr. Brown has said. If there is no limit to what he says, Christians can be hurt."

Before I could answer, my friend (and he's a good friend) felt constrained to defend me. "Wait!" he said. "I think you've misunderstood Steve. He, of course, would draw the line where you would draw the line. He isn't as loose as you think he is."

Do you know what I did? I smiled.

Later, in the hotel room, I realized that I had backed off when I shouldn't have, and I decided I wasn't going to back off anymore. No more shilly-shallying for me. You should decide to do the same thing. I'll pray for you, and you pray for me.

Will God still love you if you shilly-shally or compromise the grace and freedom he has taught you? Of course he will—but you be careful out there.

WHAT'S MOST IMPORTANT?

The Bible says,

> Have this mind among yourselves, which is yours in Christ Jesus, who, though he was in the form of God, did not count equality with God a thing to be grasped, but made himself nothing, taking the form of a servant, being born in the likeness of men. And being found in human form, he humbled himself by becoming obedient to the point of death, even death on a cross.[15]

Paul wrote: "For though I am free from all, I have made myself a servant to all, that I might win more of them."[16]

Really free people don't have to grasp their freedom to themselves. In fact, I've sometimes forgotten that my freedom isn't the most important thing in the world. On those occasions I've forgotten what great freedom and joy can be found in giving up my freedom.

> WILL GOD STILL LOVE YOU IF YOU SHILLY-SHALLY? OF COURSE HE WILL— BUT YOU BE CAREFUL OUT THERE.

Free people remain free to give up their freedom. They bestow freedom on others by giving up their own. Soldiers who fight for freedom (and who sometimes die for it) provide good models for us. Soldiers of Christ should always be willing to do that.

In *The Freedom of a Christian*, Martin Luther said, "To make the way smoother for the unlearned—for only them do I serve—I shall set down the following two propositions concerning the freedom and the bondage of the spirit: A Christian is a perfectly free lord of all, subject to none. A Christian is a perfectly dutiful servant of all, subject to all."[17]

We've spent most of this book talking about the first of those propositions, and I don't want you to forget that. Luther put it this way:

> No good work can rely upon the Word of God or live in the soul, for faith alone and the Word of God rule in the soul. Just as the heated iron glows like fire because of the union of fire with it, so the Word imparts its qualities to the soul. It is clear, then, that a Christian has all that he needs in faith and need no works to justify him; and if he has no need of works, he has no need of the law; and if he has no need of the law, surely he is free from the law.[18]

But we need to remind ourselves about the other side, the second of Luther's propositions. Listen to what Luther said (after talking about the wonderful freedom we have):

> What man is there whose heart, upon hearing these things, will not rejoice to its depth, and when receiving such comfort will not grow tender so that he will love Christ as he never could by means of any laws or works? . . . Behold, from faith thus flow forth love and joy in the Lord, and from love a joyful, willing, and free mind that serves one's neighbor willingly and takes no account of gratitude or ingratitude, of praise or blame, of gain or loss. For a man does not serve that he may put men under obligations. He does not distinguish between friend or enemies or anticipate their thankfulness or unthankfulness, but he most freely and most willingly spends himself and all that he has, whether he wastes all on the thankless or whether he gains a reward. As his Father does, distributing all things to all men richly and freely.[19]

So many people are so bound—so angry, so afraid, in such need of appearing right and righteous, so condemning, so bound by rules and regulations, so lonely, so afraid that someone will reveal their secrets, so sure that God is angry at them, so empty, in such doubt—and they can't tell anybody.

If you've read this book, you are now here for them.

Oh, and one more thing. You know all of the "be careful out there" things I just said? Delete them. Only bound people are careful.

You don't have to be.

NOTES

Introduction: Naming the Demons

1. William D. Hendricks, *Exit Interviews: Revealing Stories of Why People Are Leaving the Church* (Chicago: Moody Press, 1993), 279–80.

One: The Freedom We Surrender . . . and the Heritage That Sets Us Free

1. Romans 14:14.

2. 2 Corinthians 3:17.

3. Galatians 5:13 NRSV.

4. 1 Corinthians 8:13.

5. Romans 4:11, 22–24 KJV.

6. Psalm 73:3–9, 13.

7. Romans 2:4.

8. Matthew 23:4,15.

9. Matthew 20:26–28.

10. Matthew 20:25–26.

11. Romans 14:4.

12. Matthew 13:24–30, 47–51.

13. Associated Press, "He's a Super Man," *Hickory Daily Record*, July 1, 2000.

Two: The Gods We Worship . . . and the God Who Sets Us Free

1. Philip Yancey, *Disappointment with God* (Grand Rapids: Zondervan, 1992), 9.

2. Dan Allender and Tremper Longman, *Cry of the Soul: How our Emotions Reveal Our Deepest Questions about God* (Colorado Springs: NavPress, 1994), 142.

3. Brent Curtis and John Eldredge, *The Sacred Romance* (Nashville: Thomas Nelson, 1997), 2.

4. John 1:1–3, 14.

5. 1 John 1:1–2.

6. Hebrews 1:1–3 NKJV.

7. C. S. Lewis, *The Lion, the Witch, and the Wardrobe* (New York: Macmillan, 1950), 64–65.

8. Hebrews 10:31.

9. Psalm 50:21–22 NIV.

10. Isaiah 55:8–9.

11. Romans 11:34–36.

12. Matthew 13:41–42.

13. Matthew 11:28–30.

14. John 3:16–17.

15. John 1:12.

16. Galatians 3:26.

17. Romans 4:22–25.

18. Romans 8:1.

19. Romans 8:33–35, 37–39.

20. John 8:36.

21. Mike Mason, *Practicing the Presence of People* (Colorado Springs: WaterBrook Press, 1999), 181.

Three: The Perfection We Desire . . . and the Forgiveness That Sets Us Free

1. Bryan Chapell, *Holiness by Grace* (Wheaton, Ill.: Crossway Books, 2001), 39–40.

2. C. S. Lewis, *Mere Christianity* (New York: Macmillan, 1952), 167.

3. Romans 6:1–2, 15.

4. Psalm 119:151–52.

5. Psalm 119:97–98.

6. Galatians 3:24.

7. John 14:15–18.

8. Romans 7:15, 19.

9. Robert Kolb and David A. Lumpp, *Martin Luther: Companion to the Contemporary Christian* (St. Louis: Concordia Publishing, 1982).

Four: The Gospel We Forget . . . and the Joy That Sets Us Free

1. I Timothy 1:15.

2. Matthew 11:19; Luke 7:34.

3. Matthew 23:4.

4. Luke 4:18–19.

5. Calvin Miller, *An Owner's Manual for the Unfinished Soul* (Wheaton Ill.: Harold Shaw Publishers, 1997), 120–22.

6. Ephesians 6:25–27, 30, 32.

7. Romans 4:22–25.

8. Gerald G. May, M.D., *Addiction and Grace: Love and Spirituality in the Healing of Addictions* (San Francisco: Harper, 1991), 150.

9. Matthew 7:1–4.

10. Luke 7:47.

11. 1 Timothy 1:15.

12. Jody Vickery, "Get Thou Over It," *Christianity Today*, December 4, 2000, 82.

13. Matthew 5:20.

Five: The Masks We Wear . . . and the Authenticity That Sets Us Free

1. C. P. P. Taylor, *Good: And a Nightingale Sang* (New York: Routledge, Chapman, and Hall, 1990).

2. Revelation 3:17–18 (emphasis added).

3. Romans 12:3.

4. Harry Stein, *How I Accidentally Joined the Vast Right-Wing Conspiracy (and Found Inner Peace)* (New York: Delacorte Press/Random House, 2000), 62, 63, 68.

5. 2 Corinthians 11:1.

6. 2 Corinthians 11:16.

7. 2 Corinthians 11:17.

8. 2 Corinthians 12:1.

Six: The People We Deify . . . and the Truth That Sets Us Free

1. Jeremiah 17:9.

2. 2 Corinthians 4:7–10.

3. Acts 17:11.

4. 1 Corinthians 4:7, 9–10.

5. Harold L. Bussell, *Unholy Devotion: Why Cults Lure Christians* (Grand Rapids: Zondervan, 1983), 65.

6. Proverbs 27:17.

7. Charles and Janet Morris, *Jesus in the Midst of Success: Standing Faithful in Seasons of Abundance* (Nashville: Broadman and Holman Publishers, 2000), 47.

8. Ecclesiastes 4:9–12.

Seven: The Enemies We Demonize . . . and the Humanity That Sets Us Free

1. Matthew 8:22.

2. 1 Timothy 1:15 (emphasis added).

3. Saint John Chrysostom, *Homilies on the Epistles of Paul to the Corinthians*, Vol. XII, *Nicene and Post Nicene Fathers*, Eerdmans, 1st ser., 227 (Grand Rapids, 1978).

4. Romans 14:4–5.

5. Stein, *Right-Wing Conspiracy*, 132.

6. Romans 11:34.

7. Isaiah 55:8–9.

8. James 2:19.

9. Colossians 2:15.

10. John 16:33.

11. See Acts 7:55, 56; Romans 8:34; Colossians 3:1; Hebrews 10:12.

12. Daniel 4:35.

13. Matthew 23:4–7.

Eight: The Boldness We Fear . . . and the Courage That Sets Us Free

1. Matthew 5:13.

2. Galatians 4:30–5:1.

3. John 8:36.

4. Fant and Pinson, eds. *Twenty Centuries of Great Preaching* (Waco, Tex.: Word, 1971), 1:145.

5. David Morrison, *Beyond Gay* (Huntington, Ind.: Our Sunday Visitor Publishing, 1999).

6. Ibid., 53–54.

7. Ibid., 54.

8. Matthew 10:16–17.

9. Matthew 28:18–20.

10. 1 Corinthians 14:8–9, 23.

11. John 19:11.

12. Matthew 10:27–31.

13. Romans 8:37–39.

Nine: The Pain We Avoid . . . and the Reality That Sets Us Free

1. M. Scott Peck, M.D., *The Road Less Traveled: A New Psychology of Love, Traditional Values, and Spiritual Growth* (New York: Simon and Schuster, 1979), 17.

2. Ibid.

3. Genesis 3:16.

4. Genesis 3:17–19.

5. Romans 8:18–23.

6. John 16:33.

7. John 15:18, 20.

8. Philippians 3:8, 10.

9. Colossians 1:24.

10. Acts 9:15–16.

11. 2 Corinthians 11:23–28.

12. Philippians 1:29.

13. Jeremiah 12:5.

14. 2 Corinthians 1:8.

15. Galatians 2:11–12.

16. 1 Corinthians 15:42.

17. 2 Corinthians 1:20.

18. 1 Peter 1:6–7.

19. 1 Peter 4:12.

20. 2 Timothy 1:7.

21. Matthew 10:16.

22. Revelation 21:4.

23. 2 Corinthians 12:9.

24. 2 Corinthians 3:16–18.

Ten: The Failure We Foster . . . and the Victory That Sets Us Free

1. 2 Corinthians 5:17.

2. Romans 8:1.

3. Colossians 2:18 NIV (emphasis added).

4. Colossians 2:23 (emphasis added).

5. Psalm 19:7–8, 10–11.

6. Galatians 3:24.

7. Romans 7:24.

8. Thomas Kelly, *The Eternal Promise* (New York: Harper and Row, 1966), 23.

9. *The Majors of Golf,* 2000, The PGA Championship Edition, 36.

Eleven: The Path We Avoid . . . and the Journey That Sets Us Free

1. 1 Peter 2:16.

2. Galatians 5:13.

3. 1 Corinthians 6:12.

4. Ephesians 3:16–19.

5. 2 Timothy 1:7.

6. Psalm 34:4.

7. Isaiah 12:2.

8. 1 John 4:18.

9. 1 Peter 2:9–10.

10. John 15:14.

11. Matthew 12:49.

12. Romans 8:15.

13. Ephesians 2:14.

14. Galatians 5:1.

15. Philippians 2:5–8.

16. 1 Corinthians 9:19.

17. Timothy Lull, ed., *Martin Luther's Basic Theological Writings* (Minneapolis: Fortress Press, 1989), 586.

18. Ibid., 601.

19. Ibid., 609, 619.

For more from Steve Brown, contact Key Life Network at 1-800-KEYLIFE or www.keylife.org. Key Life is a ministry committed to getting people Home with radical freedom, infectious joy, and surprising faithfulness.